Holy
Week

Aids for Interpreting
the Lessons of the Church Year

Holy
Week

Reginald Fuller

Elizabeth Achtemeier, series editor

Series B

FORTRESS PRESS   Philadelphia

Library of Congress Cataloging in Publication Data

Fuller, Reginald Cuthbert.
   Holy Week, series B.

   (Proclamation 3)
     1. Bible—Homiletical use. 2. Bible—Liturgical
Lessons, English. 3. Holy Week. I. Title. II. Series.
BS534.5.F837 1984   220.6   84–6011
ISBN 0–8006–4104–3

Contents

Series Foreword

Proclamation 3 is an entirely new aid for preaching from the three-year ecumenical lectionary. In outward appearance this new series is similar to *Proclamation: Aids for Interpreting the Lessons of the Church Year* and *Proclamation 2*. But *Proclamation 3* has a new content as well as a new purpose.

First, there is only one author for each of the twenty-eight volumes of *Proclamation 3*. This means that each author handles both the exegesis and the exposition of the stated texts, thus eliminating the possibility of disparity between scholarly apprehension and homiletical application of the appointed lessons. While every effort was made in *Proclamation: Aids* and in *Proclamation 2* to avoid such disparity, it tended to creep in occasionally. *Proclamation 3* corrects that tendency.

Second, *Proclamation 3* is directed primarily at homiletical interpretation of the stated lessons. We have again assembled the finest biblical scholars and preachers available to write for the series; now, however, they bring their skills to us not primarily as exegetes, but as interpreters of the Word of God. Exegetical material is still presented—sometimes at length—but, most important, here it is also applied; the texts are interpreted and expounded homiletically for the church and society of our day. In this new series scholars become preachers. They no longer stand back from the biblical text and just discuss it objectively. They engage it—as the Word of God for the worshiping community. The reader therefore will not find here the divisions between "exegesis" and "homiletical interpretation" that were marked off in the two earlier series. In *Proclamation 3* the work of the pulpit is the context and goal of all that is written.

There is still some slight diversity between the several lections and calendars of the various denominations. In an effort to overcome such diversity, the North American Committee on a Common Lectionary issued an experimental "consensus lectionary" (*The Common Lec-*

7

tionary), which is now being tried out in some congregations and which will be further altered at the end of a three-year period. When the final form of that lectionary appears, *Proclamation* will take account of it. In the meantime, *Proclamation 3* deals with those texts that are used by *most* denominations on any given Sunday. It also continues to use the Lutheran numbering of the Sundays "after Pentecost." But Episcopalians and Roman Catholics will find most of their stated propers dealt with under this numbering.

Each author writes on three lessons for each Sunday, but no one method of combining the appointed lessons has been imposed upon the writers. The texts are sometimes treated separately, sometimes together—according to the author's own understanding of the texts' relationships and messages. The authors interpret the appointed texts as these texts have spoken to them.

Reginald Fuller, author of the present volume, is a distinguished New Testament scholar and professor at the Episcopal Theological Seminary in Virginia. In some respects he has gone his own way in organizing the work, but, as always, he gives us an abundance of exegetical and homiletical material.

ELIZABETH ACHTEMEIER

Sunday of the Passion
Palm Sunday

Lutheran	Roman Catholic	Episcopal	Pres/UCC/Chr	Meth/COCU
Zech. 9:9–10	Isa. 50:4–7	Isa. 45:21–25 or Isa. 52:13—53:12	Zech. 9:9–12	Zech. 9:9–12
Phil. 2:5–11	Phil. 2:6–11	Phil. 2:5–11	Heb. 12:1–6	Phil. 2:5–11
Mark 14:1—15:47 or Mark 15:1–39	Mark 14:1—15:47 or Mark 15:1–39	Mark (14:32–72) 15:1–39 (40–47)	Mark 11:1–11	Mark 14:1—15:47

It has been a surprise—and in some cases a shock—to many American Protestants to discover that the new lectionary places primary emphasis this day on the Passion rather than on the Palm Sunday entry into Jerusalem. As a matter of fact, it was only in the mid-nineteenth century or later that the palm emphasis became paramount. The new lectionary has called us back to what had always been the tradition of the Roman Missal and the Book of Common Prayer. The palm liturgy is strictly an entrance rite leading to the Passion.

FIRST LESSON: ZECHARIAH 9:9–10

The homilist can handle this reading in either of two ways. If one feels constrained in spite of what was said above to concentrate on the Palm Sunday entry as the reading of the day, one will want to focus upon this lesson to the exclusion of the other readings, leaving the Passion for Good Friday.

If we accept the historical-critical method, we can no longer believe that Second Zechariah was consciously and intentionally predicting our Lord's triumphal entry. Rather, he intended his oracle as a message to the people of Israel in the concrete historical situation of his own day. Increasingly, however, the scholarly consensus is that the prophet is not referring to a particular conqueror such as Alexander the Great but to an ideal future when God will finally triumph. God

9

will soon send his Messianic King who will enter Jerusalem, not as a warlike figure on a horse, but as the Prince of Peace riding an ass. Commentators tell us that earthly kings in the East might on ceremonial occasions in peacetime ride on an ass but in time of war ride on a horse. For an analogy we might think of a modern ruler riding in peacetime in a limousine but in wartime in a jeep.

New Testament scholars are not agreed on whether Jesus consciously and deliberately set out to model his behavior on Palm Sunday on the picture painted by Zech. 9:9–10, or whether, as John's Gospel seems to suggest, the connection occurred to the disciples only after Easter (John 12:15–16). Mark does not mention the Zechariah text, and Matthew includes it only as one of his own (redactional) fulfillment citations, thereby suggesting that it is really his own subsequent theological comment. The early Christians, it seems, not Jesus, first made the connection. And the connection is legitimate if we think of the prophecy, not as consciously predicting the coming of Jesus, but as exhibiting an insight into the ways of God that ultimately came to rest in the person and career of Jesus of Nazareth. He is the true Prince of Peace whose journey on the ass was to lead him to an even greater humiliation, described in the Philippians hymn and portrayed in the Passion reading. But, like Second Zechariah's original prophecy, this fulfillment has to be affirmed in a world in turmoil. Peace did not come to that world. Have we any more assurance that it will come to ours? The answer to this question cannot be an unqualified yes or no. On the one hand it is clear that the nations of this world and the ruling powers are as ruthless today as they were in the world for which this prophecy was first uttered. And they are armed with weapons and have behind them an industrial-military complex such as Zechariah never knew. The Christian church has no secret wisdom to decide whether unilateral nuclear disarmament or nuclear deterrent is the safest policy to avoid a nuclear holocaust, and Christians and church people are legitimately divided on that score. On the other hand Christ has come on an ass and has died on the cross. God too has vindicated him and as a result brought into being a community in which the peace that passes all understanding is already known and which has the power to set up modest advance signs of the ultimate triumph of the Prince of Peace. So the answer to our question, the answer offered by our text, is both a qualified no and a qualified yes.

If the preacher or homilist decides to use this text in subordination to the other two, it will underline the voluntary humiliation of which the epistle also speaks ("he humbled himself") and which is narrated in the Markan Passion narrative. Mark as we shall see, speaks more than any of the other Gospels, of the humble submission of Jesus to weakness, loneliness, and dereliction.

SECOND LESSON: PHILIPPIANS 2:5–11; GOSPEL: MARK 14:1—15:41

It is best to take these two readings together. The Philippians hymn provides a framework in which the passion narrative is to be understood.

What, precisely, that framework is, is a matter of controversy among New Testament scholars. Most hold that the hymn portrays a three-stage Christology. It speaks of a preexistent redeemer who descended from heaven and became incarnate (first stage), who lived a human life of perfect obedience culminating in death on a cross (second stage), and who is now exalted as universal Lord (third stage). Quite recently however two scholars have plausibly argued for a two-stage scheme here. First, Jesus is an earthly figure who reverses the role of Adam (first stage); he is then vindicated (second stage). Fortunately for our present purposes we do not have to decide between these two interpretations. On either view Jesus is presented as one who humbled himself to death on a cross. It does not make all that much difference to that humiliation whether it started with the incarnation of the preexistent one who divested himself of the glory of God or whether it is the humbling of one who started out with the dignity of being the image of God, which Adam had enjoyed before the fall. Only, the humiliation is greater if it starts from the glory in heaven. Either pattern forms a suitable background for the understanding of the Markan passion, though Mark's Christology admittedly fits in better with a two-stage Christology. For Mark knows nothing of the preexistence of the Redeemer. Moreover, it is arguable that Mark does, at least in the Temptation narrative, present Jesus as the second Adam who was with the wild beasts and who thus by his obedience restored the primordial harmony of the cosmos disrupted by Adam's fall. Yet again, even if we hold to the three-stage interpretation of the Philippian hymn, we can still see in its second stage, beginning at a later point in the hymn, an Adam Christology, namely, at the point where the hymn begins to speak of the *obedience* of the Redeemer (verse 8). Whereas Adam disobeyed and was cast out of paradise, the Christ obeyed perfectly and was ("therefore") exalted and given the name *Iesous Christos Kyrios.*

A second, much controverted problem of interpretation in this hymn is the use which Paul makes of it in Philippians. Two interpretations of v. 5 are possible: (1) "imitate the mind-set of Christ as an external example" (KJV); (2) actualize and implement the mind-set which has already been created in you by your incorporation into Christ (RSV). The way we answer this question may well decide how we are going to preach on the passion of Saint Mark's Gospel. Is Christ crucified to be set forth as an example for us to follow? There is scriptural justification for taking this line (see, for example, 1 Pet. 2:21). It is also the way today's collect in the *Book of Common Prayer,* based as it is on this epistle reading, takes it: "Almighty and everliving God, in your tender love for the human race you sent your Son our Savior Jesus Christ to take upon him our nature, and to suffer death upon the cross, giving us the example of his great humility: Mercifully grant that we may walk in the way of his suffering, and also share in his resurrection." If however we take the second interpretation, it will guide us into an understanding of the Markan passion as the redemptive act of God for us and for our salvation. That is probably a theologically more fruitful interpretation, while the former interpretation is more appealing to the practical-minded. Given the present stage of exegesis, both would seem to be legitimate interpretations.

THE MARKAN PASSION

There are four passion stories, one in each of the Gospels. The older way to read them, particularly favored in earlier Lutheran tradition, was to put them all together into a single account. Today this would seem to critical scholars to be an illegitimate harmonization. It is as a matter of fact unfair to each of the Gospel writers. The Gospels are not photographs but portraits. Each evangelist has seen something unique and caught it on his canvas, and we must allow each to speak for himself. If we want to recover what happened historically we should look rather to what is common among the evangelists and so reconstruct a primitive outline which underlies all four developed accounts. Such an outline would run something like this: Jesus was arrested, probably on the day before the Passover, and brought before the Sanhedrin, not for a trial, but for a process analogous to our grand jury proceedings. Various possible charges were put forward, such as Jesus' prediction of the destruction of the Temple, his word about the tribute money, his implied claim to a special relationship with God, a claim that involved blasphemy. But finally they settled for a political charge: Was Jesus setting himself as a messianic pretender? It was a charge which Jesus apparently neither accepted nor denied—pleading as it were the Fifth Amendment. This refusal on Jesus' part was taken by the Sanhedrin as tantamount to an admission of guilt, and it gave them a political charge of which Pilate could take cognizance. While all this was going on, Peter denied having any involvement with Jesus. The mockery scenes probably have some historical basis. The most likely setting for them was, as Luke suggests, while the Temple police were whiling away time between the arrest at night and the Sanhedrin session in the morning.

Pilate eventually found Jesus guilty and sentenced him to crucifixion on the charge of being a messianic pretender. Probably the other prisoners who were executed with him had been involved in a political insurrection. Pilate seems initially to have suspected something phoney about the charge against Jesus, but eventually he bowed to the wishes of the Sanhedrin authorities. Jesus and the two others were thereupon crucified. The *titulus* stated that he was executed as messianic pretender. Jesus expired with a loud cry, his death being unusually early. His body was thrown into a (? common) grave—perhaps the last insult against him by his enemies (Acts 13:29). This is a remarkably secular story. Except for the earlier charges discussed in the Sanhedrin there is nothing intrinsically religious about it. It acquires its religious aura and its theological significance partly from the demeanor of Jesus throughout his prior career and partly through the impact of the Easter experience upon the disciples. Jesus' prior demeanor meant that the post-Easter interpretation was not an arbitrary imposition upon the original history but was in continuity with Jesus' self-understanding and intention.

The earliest community proclaimed the death of Jesus as the people's no to God's offer of eschatological salvation and the resurrection as God's yes, his vindication of that offer. As they celebrated the Passover, the earliest Christians added to the original Jewish *anamnesis* (remembrance) of the exodus a second *anamnesis,* that of the Christ event. For this purpose they required a new Passover haggada. This would correspond to the haggada, or narrative of the original exodus, recited by the oldest person present at every seder in response to the enquiry of the youngest member, "What do you mean by this service?" (Exod. 12:26). Thus the Passion narrative took shape. The crucifixion was narrated, not as bare, secular history, but in language derived from the psalms and from prophetic books so as to picture Jesus as the righteous sufferer who was vindicated by God.

Jesus had died as a messianic pretender. His vindication by God in the resurrection meant that he really was the Messiah. He was also something unheard of, a crucified Messiah. So the passion narrative has to stress, not only that it was within the purpose of God, but that it was as Messiah that Jesus died. This was already expressed by the historical fact of the title on the cross, but the trial scenes and the mockery scenes were developed so as to further emphasize this theological truth.

At an early date, though probably not right at the beginning, the passion narrative was extended backwards from the arrest to include an account of the Last Supper. But, as Paul's inclusion of the Lord's Supper as a separate pericope in 1 Cor. 11:23–26 and the Fourth Gospel's omission of it in the account of the Last Supper both indicate, the institution of the Lord's Supper was probably not originally even a part of the extended narrative.

What then is the Markan portrait of the passion? First, we note how much more important the passion is for Mark than anything else in the story of the ministry. It occupies two long chapters to itself, compared with the brief pericopes of which the rest of the Gospel material is composed. The shadow of the cross looms over the story from the very first chapter, with its introduction of Jesus in his baptism as the (Suffering) Servant of Second Isaiah, and then more strongly after Peter's confession, which is followed by three passion predictions like the ominous tolling of a bell.

At the same time there are striking differences between the passion story and the rest of the Gospel. The earlier chapters had portrayed Jesus as one who acted with power and taught with authority. Now all that vanished. Jesus is stripped of that power, and his authoritative speech is silenced. Mark emphasizes the loneliness of Jesus in his passion. The disciples fall asleep while Jesus wrestles alone in prayer in the Garden of Gethsemane. They desert him at the moment of his arrest. Peter does indeed follow him to the High Priest's palace, but only to deny him three times. The High Priest manipulates the Sanhedrin to pronounce Jesus guilty and deserving of death. Some of the bystanders spit upon him, blindfold him, and mockingly challenge him to play the prophet. The police strike him, adding injury to insult. Before Pilate's court the crowd cries for the release of Barabbas and for the crucifixion of Jesus. The Roman soldiers dress him up as a would-be king, in a purple robe and a crown of thorns and cry out, "Hail, King of the Jews!" At Golgotha the passers-by taunt him, reminding him of how he had said he would destroy the Temple and rebuild it in three days, and they challenge him to use his vaunted power by coming down from the cross. Even two crucified with him join in the mockery—no penitent thief in Mark. There is darkness over the whole land for three hours. Finally, forsaken in the end by even God himself, when he has called *Abba*, his dear Father, Jesus cries with a loud voice: *"Eloi, Eloi, lama sabachthani?"* He dies bereft and in utter loneliness—no mother and beloved disciple at hand as in John, his kinsfolk and acquaintances standing afar off.

Yet there is another side to the passion story as told by Mark. The narrative is frequently punctuated by Old Testament allusions and occasionally by an explicit Old Testament quotation. This is to say, in all this dreadful story the reader is being told that God is really at work—even in the loneliness and dereliction of Jesus. Jesus assures the disciples at the Supper that after his death God will raise him and then he will go before them into Galilee, the place where the mission to the Gentiles will be inaugurated. That mission to the Gentiles is also foreshadowed in the (Gentile) centurion's exclamation, "Truly, this man was the Son of God!"—the only privileged person who confessed Jesus as a Messiah and got away with it, without a command to silence. Before the High Priest, Jesus confidently predicts his exaltation to the right hand of God and his coming again in glory.

This does not mean that the Passion story is a charade. It is precisely in and through the suffering and dereliction of Jesus that God is at work. Jesus really was bereft of the Father, not just reciting psalms, psalms that have a happy ending. Paul summed up in theological terms what Mark has cast in the form of a narrative: "Christ redeemed us from the curse of the law, having become a curse for us" (Gal. 3:13). And again: "For our sake he made him to be sin who knew no sin, so that in him we might become the righteousness of God."

This is what makes the cross the saving act of God. This makes it possible for us to respond to the cross in faith and to be incorporated into it, so that we can have that mindset which was in Christ Jesus and reproduce the lineaments of the passion in our own lives by humility (leaving it to God to justify us) and obedience.

The Servant Songs:
Old Testament

Each day of this week from Monday through Friday, with the exception of Maundy Thursday, we read in order one of the Servant Songs of Second Isaiah. The preacher might find it desirable to preach a course of sermons on these Songs, and so we will deal with them here as a series.

But first some introductory remarks on the Servant Songs. There are two major problems connected with them which require clarity in the preacher's mind before he can write his sermons. The first concerns the original meaning of the Songs—the question asked by the Ethiopian eunuch in Acts 8:34—"About whom, pray, does the prophet say this, about himself or about someone else?" As in the case of the Palm Sunday text from Second Zechariah, we can no longer accept the view of our forefathers expressed in the heading which the King James Version prints above Isaiah 53: "The prophet foretelleth Christ's sufferings." The prophet, writing during the exile, was addressing his contemporaries about their own historical situation. Old Testament scholars are divided about the identity of the "Servant" in that situation. It has been variously thought to be the prophet himself, some other prophet such as Jeremiah, or one of the kings of Judah as the representative and embodiment of his people, a faithful remnant of the people or the people in its entirety, or even the future Messiah. Some passages speak of the servant as Israel itself (Isa. 49:3; cf. 44:1). Others speak of the Servant as having a mission to Israel (Isa. 42:6; 49:6). It seems that the Servant is a figure capable of expansion and contraction, sometimes standing for the people as a whole, sometimes presented as one who at once personifies the people and has a mission to them. Perhaps we could best define the servant as "the bearer of God's purpose in salvation history." The prophet was given profound insights into what it means to be the bearer of God's purpose in salvation history, insights which finally came to rest in the career and fate of Jesus of Nazareth. In this sense the New Testament was justified in applying the Servant Songs to Jesus.

The second problem is, did Jesus himself make that application or was it the work of the later church? That Jesus did apply servant language to his mission is indicated by the answer to John in prison (Matt 11:5 par.) and, less certainly (for it is attested only by Luke and may be redactional), the use of Isaiah 61 in his inaugural address in the synagogue at Nazareth (Luke 4:18-21). On the other hand explicit influence of Isaiah 53 is found only in the later strata of the Gospel tradition, as in the addition to the sayings on service in Mark 10:45b, in the expansion of the cup-word in the Supper tradition at Mark 14:24, and in the (redactional) fulfillment citations in Matt. 8:17 and Luke 22:37. The earliest kerygma, like the earliest strata of the passion story, with its use of the Psalms rather than the Servant Songs seems to have presented Jesus, not as the Suffering Servant, but as the righteous sufferer who was vindicated by God. Only at a somewhat later stage, with the introduction of the *hyper* ("for," "on our behalf" see 1 Cor. 15:3) formula are there suggestions of Isaiah 53. We seem to be led to the conclusion that it was only in somewhat later reflection on the early community's part that the specific notion of the Suffering Servant, whose sufferings had an atoning significance, emerged as an interpretation of Jesus' career and fate. This does not mean that the application was illegitimate, for the Spirit was given to lead the church into all truth. But it does mean that the preacher must be aware that in referring the Servant Songs to Jesus he is giving an interpretation, not recounting historic fact.

MONDAY IN HOLY WEEK:
ISAIAH 42:1–9 (SONG 1)

Song 1 falls into two parts (vv. 1–4 and vv. 5–9). In part 1 we have the initial designation of the Servant. First, he is chosen and elected for his role in salvation history (v. 1a, b). Then he is equipped for that role (v. 1c). His role is described in 1d, 3c, and 4b as the bringer of righteousness (or salvation), and in 4a it is promised ultimate success.

In part 2 Yahweh speaks without direct reference to the Servant, repeating the substance of the first part (call, equipment, description of role, and promise of success), but adding to it a reference to the covenant and to the universal scope of the salvation the Servant will bring (v. 6).

This song will provide the preacher with an opportunity to outline Jesus' healing ministry before his passion and to show how the passion was not just an unfortunate accident at the end of his career, an absurdity unrelated to it (for example as Camus's death on a motorbike was unrelated to his previous career), but a culmination of that ministry. From the very moment of his baptism (which is narrated in the gospels in the language of this first Servant Song) Jesus was moving toward the cross. His healings were advance signs of the salvation that was to be accomplished there.

In order to give this text a contemporary application, the preacher may wish to show how the servant church continues the Servant's work today, opening the eyes of the blind and bringing liberation to those imprisoned in various kinds of existential bondage.

TUESDAY IN HOLY WEEK:
ISAIAH 49:1–6 (SONG 2)

This song is addressed to the foreign nations by the Servant himself, and he reports what Yahweh had said to him. It has a threefold pattern. In vv. 1b–3 the Servant speaks of his election, call, and equipment (cf. Song 1). In v. 4 he speaks of his despondency at the apparent failure of his mission. Then in v. 6 he is given a new mission, not just to Israel, but to the nations and to the end of the earth.

Failure seems to be a regular concomitant of the prophetic mission: witness Moses, Elijah, and Jeremiah. But Yahweh vindicates his prophets and turns their failure into opportunity for new service. That too was the constant experience of Jesus, culminating in the failure of the cross. But God delivered him out of that failure and through it founded a new community that was to embark upon a universal mission.

The preacher will want to dwell upon the Lord's failure, culminating on the cross, and how for him that failure was the necessary condition for the successful accomplishment of his mission. He may then apply these insights into the life of the Christian church today. On the one hand we tend to evaluate our success in superficial, worldly ways (expanding congregations, budgets, and building programs), and on the other we tend to be easily discouraged in the face of apparent failure. Fidelity to mission—with the possibility and even certainty of the cross—rather than outward success is the criterion by which the church is to be evaluated.

WEDNESDAY IN HOLY WEEK:
ISAIAH 50:4-9 (SONG 3)

Of all the Servant Songs this is the easiest to understand. Its form is that of lament. Once again, the Servant is suffering as a bearer of the word of God. The assaults he must endure are grievous. But in vv. 7–9 the Servant affirms his confidence in the help and vindication of Yahweh.

The new feature of this song is that the servant uncomplainingly submits to the insults and injuries he has to endure—a definite advance on Jeremiah, for instance, who complained bitterly. Another interesting feature about it is the picture of the prophet waiting every morning to receive a new word from Yahweh. Both of these features closely foreshadow the career of Jesus. He, too, willingly and uncomplainingly submitted to injury and insult in the trial scenes. He, too, as presented in the Gospel of John, was constantly hearing his Father's words and passing them on to his opponents and his disciples (for example, John 5:19–20).

The preacher may want to use this song to bring out the connection between the discourses of Jesus in the Fourth Gospel and the passion. It is because Jesus brings from God a revelation his contemporaries cannot bear that he is rejected and brought to the cross. So too the church as the servant today must live in constant prayer and in meditation upon Scripture and so receive from him the words with which to sustain "those who are weary," and she must be ready like her Master to be rejected and persecuted by those who refuse to hear. Yet like her Master she must realize that she has the divine assistance and the certainty of vindication.

GOOD FRIDAY:
ISAIAH 52:13—53:12 (SONG 4)

This hymn will be easier to grasp if it is divided into three sections: 52:13–15, What God says (the vindication of the servant); 53:1–11a, What others say (the Servant's sufferings and Yahweh's intervention); 53:11b–12, What God says (the saving consequences of Yahweh's intervention). Thus there are two major themes, suffering and vindication.

Just as the first song presented the beginning of the Servant's career, so the fourth song deals with its culmination. In fact, the Servant Songs provide the preacher with an opportunity of presenting the whole career of Jesus in a course extending from the baptism, on Monday, through the ministry, on Tuesday and Wednesday, to the passion and death, on Friday. The ministry gives meaning to the passion.

A new element introduced in the fourth song that makes it different from all others is that the Servant's sufferings are vicarious and expiatory. It was undoubtedly reflection on this fourth servant song that led the early church to understand Jesus' death as an atoning sacrifice. Jesus himself had at the Last Supper spoken of his death as the decisive event leading to the inauguration of the kingdom of God and of the new covenant. The message of the atonement was an explication of these sayings with the aid of the fourth servant song. "Poured out for many" was added to "blood of the covenant" (Mark 14:24).

Many theologians and others in recent times have felt uncomfortable about the use of the word *vicarious* in connection with Christ's atoning death and have preferred to speak of it as representative. Others have just as vigorously defended it. The term *vicarious* is certainly justified in the light of Isaiah 53. The servant had to suffer alone. He was there where the others should have been but could not be, for they had gone astray. The commentators on Isaiah seem to have no compunction in using the term *vicarious* in that context. But can it be applied to the death of *Christ?* Those who object to it do so because they think that there is something immoral about the notion. Christ accepts and endures the punishment while we go scot-free— the notion of penal substitution. But the clause "while we go scot-free" is an inference from *vicarious* and not a necessary inference at that. Already the Servant Songs, with their expansion from the individual to the collective, suggest that as well as being a vicarious figure the Servant is also a representative one. He goes where we should but cannot but goes so that we, too, might go after him. The death of Christ is not something external to us. We are caught up into it, incorporated into it through faith and baptism. We share his cross by dying to the old self and by being set upon the path to resurrection. Thus it seems true to say that the death of Christ, while primarily vicarious, is also secondarily representative.

The effect of the cross can be illustrated by two examples. One comes from Eduard Schweizer, the other, from C. S. Lewis. Eduard Schweizer has related how when he was a small boy vacationing up in the Alps his father would take him across the glacier where the snow was too deep for a child to walk. His father would go ahead, carving out deep footprints in the snow in which the boy could tread and so follow easily. At first the father's action was vicarious—young Eduard was too small, and the father had to go first, alone. But then the son was, as it were, caught up into the action of the father and enabled to walk where the father had first carved the way. The action of the father was at first vicarious but then also representative. C. S. Lewis's example is of a child too small and unable as yet to write. The parent places a large hand over the child's own small one and makes the letters for it, yet the child's hand is caught up into the hand of the parent and so in a way writes in and with the parent. Again, the parent's action is at once vicarious and representative.

Monday in Holy Week

Lutheran	Roman Catholic	Episcopal	Pres/UCC/Chr	Meth/COCU
Isa. 42:1–9	Isa. 42:1–7	Isa. 42:1–9	Isa. 50:4–10	Isa. 42:1–9
Heb. 9:11–15		Heb. 11:39—12:3	Heb. 9:11–15	Heb. 9:11–15
John 12:1–11	John 12:1–11	John 12:1–11 or Mark 14:3–9	Luke 19:41–48	John 12:1–11

It might in some instances be possible to link the epistle reading with either the Old Testament or the Gospel readings, but such attempts are often artificial and sometimes it seems best to take each of the readings by itself. This gives the preacher three different choices for each day. One can leave the unused possibilities for other years. Where it seems possible however, we will suggest a connection.

SECOND LESSON: HEBREWS 9:11–15

These verses form the very core of the argument of the Epistle to the Hebrews. They summarize the high priestly work of Christ and the effects of his sacrificial death. In earlier chapters the author has carefully prepared the ground for this statement by demonstrating that Jesus satisfies all the external requirements of high priesthood, that the old, Levitical high priesthood was imperfect, and that their high priestly work was ineffectual to achieve the real goal of worship: to take away sin and to enable the worshipers to draw near to God.

Our pericope consists of three sentences. The first sentence (vv. 11–12) speaks of the inauguration of the eschatological high priest, the second (vv. 13–14) of the subjective soteriological consequences of his high priestly work, and the third (v. 15) of its objective soteriological consequences. We will comment upon each of these three sentences in turn.

First, the inauguration: Here the preacher will concentrate on the sacrifice of Christ per se. He may take up the contrast between Christ's sacrifice and the old Levitical sacrifices, extending them perhaps to cover all human religion. Human religion is a quest for God which can never bring us into complete and perfect communion with God because it cannot remove the barrier of sin. Only Christ has done that by the event of the cross, by his own "blood." The gospel's claim to universality and finality is not narrow parochialism—that "our" religion is better than others—but is due to its event character, its once-for-allness.

In contrast to the work of the Levitical high priests, that of Christ takes place in a transcendent realm. He passes into a tent which is superior in three ways: (1) it is greater and more perfect; (2) it is not made with hands; (3) it is not of this creation. This tent is the way through to the holy place. Our author, it seems, holds an apocalyptic notion that there are three heavens: (1) this creation (1:10–12); (2) the heavens through which Christ passes (4:14; 9:11–12); (3) the holy place, the actual dwelling place of God, the place of the divine presence. If the scene is transcendent, so too is the offering. The Levitical priests had offered the blood of animals. Christ offered his own blood, that is, his own life surrendered in death, an act of perfect obedience to the Father's saving purpose (10:5–7). For the event of offering "blood," see also v. 14b.

In the author's perspective, the Christian day of atonement is not Good Friday alone but Good Friday and Ascension Day combined. Not only the death of Christ, but his passing into the presence of God "with his own blood" are integral parts of the messianic sacrifice. It includes both Calvary and exaltation. One can understand why the primitive church celebrated the Christian Passover as a unitary feast, rather than separating Good Friday, Easter Day, and Ascension Day into separate occasions. The fact that the church has not seen fit to reintegrate the paschal feast makes it all the more imperative to see Good Friday, Easter Day, and Ascension Day as *theologically* one. In this season we are not just commemorating historical events; we are participating in a single, integrated mystery.

Second, the subjective consequences: Verses 13–14 suggest a treatment of Christian worship—serving the living God. Christian worship is not just approaching God with praise out of the blue or in the abstract. It is a response to the gospel of the Christ event which has removed the barrier of sin. Christian worship is offered in the context of recalling (in the dynamic biblical sense of the word) Christ's saving deed. This recalling is done in the preaching and in the recital of the great thanksgiving. It leads into communion with God through Christ. But in turn such worship has to be carried out into the everyday—we are bidden to "Go in peace" and to "love and serve the Lord."

The salvific consequences of Christ's work were already in view in the first sentence of our pericope. The "good things" are eschatological realities, the realization now of what was hoped for in the past. Christ has won for us an eternal (that is, eschatological) redemption. These good things are defined subjectively—that is, in terms of their consequences in our lives. Their purpose is to purify our consciences from dead works and to enable us to serve the living God. Dead works are not just moral sins, transgressions of the divine law. All works, even acts externally conforming to the law, are dead. For sin basically means not wrongdoing but separation from God, and it is possible to do good works in separation from God, and such good works are still the works of fallen humanity. They are dead.

The author of Hebrews defines the Christian life, the life of those whose sin has been atoned for by Christ's sacrifice, primarily in terms of worship. For him, worship is access to the presence of God and communion with him. It is the goal of all religion. And the focal point of this access is liturgy. The point is well taken so long as we remember

what Ernst Käsemann calls "the worship of every day" and what
Bishop John A. T. Robinson calls "liturgy come to life." With such
sentiments the author of Hebrews would agree, as he shows in the
ethical exhortation in chapter 13.

Third, the objective consequences: Christ's death inaugurates a
new covenant with the people of God. In Christian usage the image of
the covenant had its origin in early tradition, for Jesus himself at the
Last Supper had spoken of his death as establishing a covenant. This
is shown not only by the cup word (1 Cor. 11:25; Mark 14:24) but also
by the saying in Luke 22:29, where the Greek word for *assign* is
cognate with *diathēkē,* covenant. The apostle Paul, too, had developed the theme of the new covenant (2 Cor. 3:6ff.). The image goes
back to the eschatological promise of Jer. 31:31. Salvation in the New
Testament is not just an individual matter ("Christ died for me";
"Jesus is my personal savior."). Its effect is to bring into being a new
people of God.

GOSPEL: JOHN 12:1–11

The first thing we notice as we read the Johannine account of the
anointing at Bethany is that in this Gospel it takes place on the eve of
Palm Sunday, rather than during Holy Week, as in Mark. We are
however familiar with the propensity of John to shift scenes to earlier
points in the narrative. For instance, the cleaning of the Temple has
been shifted to near the beginning of the ministry, while, as Raymond
E. Brown has shown, various features of the examination of Jesus
before the Sanhedrin have been shifted to earlier dialogues between
Jesus and the "Jews." Under the circumstances it would seem that
John is similarly responsible for shifting the anointing to its present
position and that in the pregospel tradition it had appeared in a similar
position to that which it occupies in Mark. The verbal similarities
between John and Mark are also closer here than in most other
pericopes which they share in common. This hardly argues for John's
dependence upon or even acquaintance with our canonical Mark. But
it may argue, as has recently been contended in Germany, for John's
use of the same *pre-Markan* Passion narrative as Mark himself has
used.

John has shifted the context of the scene to bring it closer to the
raising of Lazarus, the last significant episode in which Jesus was
involved. John underlines this connection between the two episodes

with the statement that the anointing took place in Bethany "where Lazarus was, whom Jesus has raised from the dead" (12:1). He then goes out of his way to note that Lazarus was one of those who were at table, although Lazarus does not otherwise play any part in the story. Then the evangelist notes that the fragrance of the ointment "filled the whole house." This is probably a piece of the symbolism of which John is so fond, especially in the Passion narrative.

What clues do these additions to the narrative offer for the evangelist's interpretation of the anointing? The raising of Lazarus was a symbol of the revelation of Jesus as the resurrection and the life. Mary had not received this revelation, as Martha had done. But now she performs an act of devotion which quite unconsciously points forward to Jesus' death, through which he will implement and effectualize his declaration to her sister that he was the resurrection and the life, and this effectualization will be universal in scope.

The redactional interpretation which the Fourth Evangelist has provided for this episode furnishes the preacher with an opportunity to link the epistle and Gospel readings together in a way which makes possible a proclamation of redemptive significance of the cross.

In his sacrificial death Jesus opens up a way of access to the presence of God by removing the barrier of sin. Thus he makes resurrection and life available to the whole world.

Tuesday in Holy Week

Lutheran	Roman Catholic	Episcopal	Pres/UCC/Chr	Meth/COCU
Isa. 49:1–6	Isa. 49:1–6	Isa. 49:1–6	Isa. 42:1–9	Isa. 49:1–9a
1 Cor. 1:18–25		1 Cor. 1:18–31	1 Tim. 6:11–16	1 Cor. 1:18–31
John 12:20–36	John 13:21–33, 36–38	John 12:37–38, 42–50 or Mark 11:15–19	John 12:37–50	John 12:37–50

SECOND LESSON: 1 CORINTHIANS 1:18–25

The first part of 1 Corinthians, which runs through chapter 6, is Paul's response to the news of affairs in the Corinthian community brought by Chloe's people (1 Cor. 1:11). Chloe may have been a wealthy woman in whose villa the local Christian community held its weekly assemblies for worship. This gave her a good opportunity to observe what was going on, and so she passed on this information to Paul, who by this time had left Corinth for Ephesus.

The first matter Chloe's people reported about was the divisions within the community. Different groups were appealing to different founders—perhaps missionaries who had personally baptized them. They claimed to belong to Paul's, Cephas's, or Apollos's party, while perhaps others were claiming to be a nonparty group ("I am of Christ") and thereby being just as partisan as the others! (Another way of taking the phrase "I am of Christ," favored by some commentators, is to treat it as a Pauline interjection: "*I* will have none of your parties, *I* belong only to Christ.") Paul's first move against this partisanship is a practical one. He had in fact baptized very few of the Corinthians, so no one could say that baptism had set up a special relationship between the minister of baptism and the candidate. (This does not mean that Paul did not regard baptism as important; what was important about it, though, was not the outward sign or act but its inner significance, what God did through it). Now Paul moves to a more theological argument. Evidently the Christians at Corinth regarded their baptism as an acquisition of wisdom, or *gnosis* (spiritual knowledge), of the information that they were of heavenly origin. They thought Christ was a minister of information rather than of transformation.

This leads Paul to draw a fundamental contrast between human wisdom (which the Corinthians were so keen on) and the Christian message. That message is focused on the cross. Actually, vv. 18–31 look very much like a typical rabbinic sermon preached on a text, which is given at the end: "Let him who boasts, boast of the Lord" (v. 31). The Corinthians were boasting of their own wisdom (perhaps this is not quite fair since they would have claimed that they had *received* it in baptism, but whatever they had received they had by their behavior, particularly boasting and elitism, treated as a purely human brand of wisdom). The message of the cross of course is nonsense to those who are on their way to destruction, to the ordinary natural human being without faith. It is merely the report of a political execution, a travesty of justice perhaps, but without any existential relevance for those who were not there at the time. It speaks of an event that apparently belongs exclusively to the past. But to those who have faith, to those who have appropriated it into their own lives, and who are therefore on the road to salvation (note that Paul says *sōzomenois*, "being saved," not *sōtheisin*, "have been saved"; Paul could never have asked the question "Are you saved?" Christians are always only in via—to such people it is the very power of God unto salvation. Notice Paul's high sacramental concept of preaching. The power of God is at work in it, for preaching makes the event of the cross a salvific reality. Paul could have said—and the logic of his argument really required that he say—that the preaching of the cross was the *wisdom* of God. But for the moment the apostle avoids the word *wisdom:* it was in bad odor in view of the situation at Corinth.

Then, like a typical rabbinic preacher, Paul goes on to show that he has the Old Testament on his side. So in v. 19 he quotes from the Septuagint (Greek) text of Isa. 29:14. This shows that God has no particular respect for human wisdom, which at Corinth had set itself up against the message of the cross.

Then, in a series of further Old Testament allusions Paul argues (v. 20) that God has in fact shown up the wisdom of this age and of this world (that is, the wisdom of ordinary human nature) for what it is, the arrogant self-assertion of humanity.

But after all, Paul will not allow the Corinthians a monopoly of the word *wisdom.* He can use it in a good sense, too. *Wisdom* can be used to denote God's plan in salvation history. God had providentially planned that the world should not attain to a knowledge of him through its own wisdom so that the true wisdom might come from him, through the message of the cross received in faith. Note the difference between the two wisdoms. Human wisdom seeks to reach up to God and when it thinks it has found him, it prides itself in arrogance about a knowledge which is in fact no knowledge at all. But the true wisdom "comes from above" as James put it. God initiates it and has done so through the cross and has actualized it in the present through the preaching. True wisdom is not humanity's search for God but God's search for humanity. Such is the wisdom mediated through the preaching of the Christian message.

In vv. 22–24 we get Paul's most brilliant description of the contrast between the world and the gospel. The Jews—they stand for the world of religion—seek signs. They refuse to take God on trust, and they ask for his credentials. This attitude is outwardly religious, but in the last analysis it is skeptical and egotistical. God must submit himself to human judgment! The Greeks on the other hand—the world of academia, the intellectuals, the philosophers and scientists—pretend to have a knowledge of ultimate truth and reality. Both Jews and Greeks, both the religious person and the skeptical academic, think that the way to the truth is a way from humanity to the truth, whereas the proper way, that revealed on the cross, is the way from the truth to humanity, from God to the world. Whether we recognize the cross as the truth depends, not on our action, but on God's call (and then on our own response in itself). We can believe, but first we have to be called. Then the cross is seen and known to be God's power and God's wisdom—a gnostic term Paul can now pick up and use but with a different meaning, from above to below instead of from below to above. The last verse of our pericope (though not, as we have seen, the end of the sermon, for that goes on to v. 31) underlines the paradox.

GOSPEL: JOHN 12:20-36

This is one of those characteristically Johannine pericopes which start out as an incident and trail off into discourse material. The Greeks who set it in motion are completely forgotten along the way.

Since these particular Greeks *(Hellēnes)* had come up to Jerusalem for the Passover, they were presumably already proselytes. Had they been Jews from abroad they would have been called *Hellēnistai*. They approach Philip (one of the disciples who in John's Gospel is assigned a minor role), doubtless because he had a Greek name and would have spoken Greek. Jesus however makes no move toward the Greeks. They cannot see him because his hour is not yet come. Note how John, for all his developed theology, is rooted in the authentic Jesus tradition. One of the most ancient features of Jesus' ministry in the synoptic Gospels was that he confined his ministry to all intents and purposes to his own people. Contacts with Gentiles were rare and strictly exceptional. Only three such episodes are recorded in the gospel tradition: Mark 7:24–30 and par., Matt. 8:5–13 and par., and our present pericope. In all of them there is an apparent barrier or impediment preventing Jesus from consorting with Gentiles freely, and in both the Mark and the Matthean stories it is *faith* that breaks down the barrier.

John's story about the Greeks at the feast recognizes the same barrier by not allowing Jesus to have direct contact with the visitors at all. Instead he makes an enigmatic parabolic pronouncement: "Unless a grain of wheat falls into the earth and dies, it remains alone; but if it dies it bears much fruit." The law of nature is the law also in the realm of the spirit: if the Greeks are to "see Jesus," that is, establish contact with the eschatological reality that is in him—they must first die, first cease to be what they are: fallen humanity cut off from the life of God. They must lose this old life in order to acquire eternal life—which was the real and only purpose of "seeing" Jesus. And they can die only when the Son of man has been glorified. For only he can die the death that needs to be died because every death of ours is still the death of fallen men and women incapable of overcoming death. Only he accordingly can be glorified or rise again unto righteousness. But when he has done that, others too can follow him—not by copying an external example, but by being drawn into his death in order to share his resurrection. That is why the Greeks cannot see Jesus now.

John did not speak of faith: the synoptists did not speak of death and resurrection. But there is no contradiction. Both John and the synoptists are really saying the same thing. Faith is not just a subjective attitude. Faith is the response to eschatological reality. That reality was already proleptically at work in the ministry of Jesus, particularly in his healings. The synoptics, beginning with Mark, link these healings with the passion. John on the other hand speaks primarily of the objective reality: "The hour has come for the Son of man to be glorified." But he, too, recognizes that subjective response is required for an appropriation of the objective reality, for a person must "follow me." And by that following Christ's servant will participate in him and in his life out of death: "Where I am, there shall my servant be also." The objective reality, the coming of salvation through the death and glorification of the Son of man, and the subjective response, following him and being incorporated into him (to substitute a Pauline metaphor for the Johannine metaphor of "being with" Jesus)—all this must happen before the Greeks can see Jesus.

The pericope might have ended at this point. But we are left puzzled as to why it was the Greeks, the non-Jews, who were selected for this special treatment of being told (by implication) that they could not "see Jesus." To answer our puzzlement John introduces what looks like a fusion of two separate scenes from the synoptic tradition:

Gethsemane and the transfiguration, the prayer of Jesus and the voice from heaven. This is to show, ostensibly to the crowd, but in reality to John's readers, that the hour appointed by God for the glorifying of the Son of man has indeed come as Jesus had asserted in v. 23. This provides the opportunity for Jesus to make the climactic statement of both paragraphs, the real answer to the quest of the Greeks: "I, when I am lifted up, will draw all men to myself." And as the evangelist comments, Jesus said this to signify the kind of death he was to die. He was to be "lifted up"—a phrase which in the typical Johannine manner has a double meaning, to be lifted up on a cross *and* to be exalted to heaven. In both of these the Son of man will be glorified. Through dying to the old human life, which he had taken to himself, he would break through to the new life, and then draw all men and women after him. The Gentiles must wait for that to happen before they can "see Jesus." The barrier which in Mark and Matthew was proleptically broken by the faith must be entirely removed before "all" can see Jesus.

The pericope closes with two verses which appear—again in typically Johannine way—to have little to do with the foregoing. They are a warning to walk while there is light, for the daylight will soon fade and darkness will fall. This warning is addressed to the crowd—not to the Greeks, who are forgotten by this time—and refers to the crowd's immediate situation. Jesus is soon going to leave them, and they will lose their chance to respond to his message. But it applied equally to the Greeks after the Son of man is glorified. They will receive the light through the preaching of the kerygma. But for John the time is short, and it is overshadowed by the imminent parousia, as the Christian mission always is in the New Testament.

The preacher will notice an obvious point of connection between the epistle reading and the Gospel. The Greeks appear in both. The cross is folly to the Greeks, and it is the Greeks who come to Jesus but cannot see him until his death on the cross and his subsequent glorification. The Greeks, as we suggested in our comment on the epistle reading, stand for the intellectuals: the academics, philosophers, and scientists. They believe that it is their task to "see Jesus," that is, to attain to ultimate truth. They believe they can do this through their own studies. The Gospel, however, tells them that they must first die, like a grain of wheat. They must abandon the notion that ultimate reality is something they can discover and master for themselves.

Their province, to be sure, is to discover and master penultimate realities. But they must allow ultimate truth to come to them from the outside, as it came in the incarnation and the cross of Christ and comes now in the preaching of the church. They must allow the cross of Christ to draw them to him and thus enable them to follow him and be where he is, to be incorporated into him and share that life to which he in his humanity has broken through. Greeks have to die in order to see Jesus, and they can only die in him who first died the death that all must die.

Wednesday in Holy Week

Lutheran	Roman Catholic	Episcopal	Pres/UCC/Chr	Meth/COCU
Isa. 50:4–9a	Isa. 50:4–9	Isa. 50:4–9a	Isa. 52:13—53:12	Isa. 50:4–9
Rom. 5:6–11		Heb. 9:11–15, 24–28	Rom. 5:6–11	Rom. 5:6–11
Matt. 26:14–25	Matt. 26:14–25	John 13:31–35 or Matt. 26:1–5, 14–25	Luke 22:1–16	John 13:21–38 or Matt. 26:1–5, 14–25

SECOND LESSON: ROMANS 5:6–11

It has long been customary to interpret chapters 5—8 of Romans in terms of four freedoms:

chapter 5—freedom from wrath

chapter 6—freedom from sin

chapter 7—freedom from the law

chapter 8—freedom from death

This neat schema has recently been trenchantly and in my view convincingly criticized by J. Christiaan Beker of Princeton. According to Beker, Paul is enunciating certain themes in 5:1–11 which he will develop in chapter 8. From 5:12 through chapter 7, he pauses to clear away certain objections that suggest themselves before embarking on those themes.

In our present pericope, vv. 6–8 enunciate the theme of the "love" that is behind justification, (the theme of the preceding section), while vv. 9–11 deal with the theme of the "already" of justification as pointing forward to its ultimate consummation.

In vv. 6–8, the Christ event intervenes at the point at which humanity is "weak." That weakness was expounded in Rom. 1:18 through 3:20. All—Jews and Gentiles alike—have sinned and fallen short of the glory of God. We have no power of ourselves to help ourselves, as the ancient collect says. God demands righteousness of us, but every time we do a righteous act this is a deed of fallen humanity, a deed still done within the state of sin. That this is so is exhibited in the fact that our righteousness, done in our fallen state, is always to some degree self-righteousness. Of that self-righteousness the Pharisee in the Gospels is the typical example as is the Jew in Paul's Romans. But even if we are Gentiles we must allow ourselves to be identified completely with the Pharisee and the Jew, for *all* have sinned, ourselves included. In that situation Christ died for the "ungodly," that is to say all "weak" human beings. It makes no difference whether we are religious or irreligious prior to justification. Even the religious person, as long as he or she is out of relation with God, is, in Paul's sense of the word, ungodly.

The Christ event occurred "at the right time" *(kata kairon).* Salvation history consists of a series of *kairoi,* decisive moments when God acts. God's act in Christ was "in the fullness of time" (Gal. 4:4), when all the other acts preparatory to it had taken place: creation, the fall, the choice of Abraham, the exodus, the giving of the law, the establishment and the destruction of the Davidic monarchy, the exile, the restoration, Alexander the Great and the dispersion in Hellenistic times, the growth of the messianic hope and of apocalyptic expectation. All this had to happen or develop before the Christ event could be properly accepted or proclaimed.

Paul contrasts God's act in Christ with ordinary human behavior. One human being might die for another if there is something worth dying for in that person—righteousness or better still, goodness—at any rate, something attractive. Paul evidently thinks of goodness as something more attractive than righteousness. We have all known people who were absolute paradigms of moral probity and yet there was something harsh about their virtue. They meticulously observe all the ethical proprieties. But they are not warm, outgoing, or sensitive. Perhaps we are like that ourselves but cannot see it. Goodness means that one is righteous with those additional qualities of caring, warmth, and sensitivity. If there was something attractive like this another might conceivably die for that person. But this is not the way we are in God's eyes. We do not have any of these qualities: no righteousness, no goodness in God's eyes that could make him want to give his Son to die for us.

Paul has not introduced the word *love* up to this point, but it must have been at the back of his mind when he was talking about human beings dying for others. Perhaps Paul knew the proverbial saying used by the Johannine Christ, "Greater love has no man than this, that a man lay down his life for his friends" (John 15:13). Perhaps, on the other hand, he shrinks from applying the word *love* to human behavior in such circumstances. Anders Nygren may have exaggerated in a one-sided way when he said that it is the quintessence of *agape* that it is not caused by any attractiveness on the part of the object, but that comes pretty close to what Paul is saying about God's agape in this particular context. Paul takes his understanding of agape from the event of the cross. Love for him is essentially, not a quality, but an event, something that happened. Although, when formulated in this sharply focused way, this is something new in the Bible, it is nevertheless congruous with Israel's earlier experience of Yahweh. In the Old Testament God's agape is above all his *hesed,* his covenant love. God effectuated his *hesed* by his choice and election of Israel to be his people, that is, it was essentially an event: he loved Israel's forebears, and brought her out of Egypt, and led her through the wilderness, and gave her the land (cf. Deut. 4:37; 8:2–10).

"God is love" is not a general truth. Sir Edwyn Hoskyns was fond of saying that this great affirmation came only at the end of the New Testament in one of its latest documents, "after all the turmoil of the Epistle to the Romans." It is only something we can affirm as a confession of faith after we have been confronted with the event of the cross and have wrestled with its meaning. Similarly, Charles Wesley's hymn "Jesus, lover of my soul" is not a mere expression of sentimentality but is all about justification:

> Plenteous grace with thee is found,
> Grace to cover all my sin.

The word translated *shows* in Rom. 5:8 is noteworthy in this connection. It does not mean that the Christ event simply illustrates for us the general truth that God is love. It means that God actualizes and effectuates his love. We can speak of the love of God or of God as love only because and only in response to the event of the cross.

Vv. 9–11 form a new stage in the argument. The opening clause, "Since we are justified by his blood," sums up the results of vv. 6–8. Christ's death was first and foremost an objective event: He died for us. But it has to be subjectively appropriated (through faith, as we know from 3:31—4:25). We accept it as "for us" and thereby participate in its effects in our own lives. As a result of his self-giving love expressed in his sacrifice of his life we are "justified," that is, brought into a right relationship with God. Not that we are at once ethically "righteous," of course. In ourselves we are still weak, ungodly, sinners, enemies (v. 10). But half the battle has been won. The "already" of our justification carries with it assurance of its consummation: "we shall be saved from his wrath." We shall be saved by his life and we can only rejoice.

Paul now introduces a new word: *reconciliation*. It means intrinsically much the same as the word *justification*. But whereas *justification* is a metaphor drawn from the law courts and denotes one's status vis à vis the law, *reconciliation* is a metaphor derived from the field of personal relationships. People have a quarrel, but then they become reconciled. The change of metaphor is helpful because it brings home to us that what is at stake in justification is a right relationship with God. It is as "enemies" that we are reconciled to God, whereas it is as unrighteous in the sight of the law that we are justified. It has recently been argued that reconciliation rather than justification should be taken as the center of Pauline theology. But from this verse it looks as though reconciliation is introduced as a secondary clarification of justification.

It is by Christ's resurrection life that we shall ultimately be saved (v. 10). In chapters 8 and 10 Paul will elaborate this. Not until the final consummation shall we partake of Christ's resurrection. Meanwhile, we have continually to rise to newness of life. Hence by implication there is something that has to happen in between our initial justification (or reconciliation) and our final salvation, namely, a constant rising to newness of life in Christ by ethical endeavor. There is a life to be lived, a life *we* have to live. Yet paradoxically (the paradox of grace) it is a life lived by us in him and by him in us: "It is no longer I who live, but Christ who lives in me." *Simul justus et peccator*, "at once righteous and a sinner" is only the beginning of the story. The *peccator* must become *justus*.

The New Oxford Annotated Bible comments on our passage "Paul never speaks of a reconciliation of God to us: it is we who are estranged." That is true of what Paul says. But we may still insist that what Paul says also implies in a certain sense that God is reconciled to us as well. For before justification we were under his *wrath;* now, through justification, we know his *love* in the event of the cross. The change from wrath to love on the part of God suggests that there is some truth in the assertion that God, too, was reconciled to us. Only—and Paul is emphatic about that—the cross is not an act of Christ against the Father, it is an act of the Father in and through Christ: *"God* shows his love in that while we were yet sinners Christ died for us." We cannot throw overboard the Reformation doctrine that Christ died to reconcile the Father with us, but we must be careful to avoid any suggestion that the Father and the Son were at cross-purposes. Calvary was not an act of the Son alone, seeking to change the attitude of the Father from wrath to love. Rather, it was an act done by the Father through and in the Son, making it possible for his previously negative relation to us to become a positive one. We are talking, not of an attitude of God or of a change of that attitude, but of a relationship between God and humanity. Calvary has changed that relationship.

GOSPEL: MATTHEW 26:14–25

The lectionary is evidently making an attempt to provide Gospel readings which cover the events in each of these days in Holy Week. Although it is not stated that the events covered by this excerpt actually occurred on Wednesday of this week, and although the Last Supper occurred on Thursday, Matthew (following Mark) certainly places them prior to the Institution narrative, which will be read tomorrow.

Our excerpt contains three matters: the compact of Judas, the preparation for the Passover, and the unmasking of Judas during the Last Supper.

Matthew has made a few changes to his Markan model. He has altered the story so that Judas himself asks for money. In Mark it was the idea of the Sanhedrin to offer Judas money to betray Jesus. This is evidence of a trend in the gospel tradition to blacken the character of Judas. He is presented by Matthew as motivated by cupidity and greed. John's Gospel exhibits the same trend, developed a little further by stigmatizing Judas as a thief (see Tuesday's Gospel). Mark simply says that the chief priests *promised* to give Judas an unspecified sum of money. Matthew has them contract for the payment on the spot and specifies the amount—thirty pieces of silver. The figure is clearly based on Zech. 11:12. We have already encountered the influence of this chapter of Second Zechariah on the development of the Passion narrative. Peripheral details of the narrative have been introduced from the desire to secure the fulfillment of prophecy. But this affects only the peripheral details. Such a basic event as the betrayal of Jesus by one of his inner circle of disciples was so scandalous that it is inconceivable it could have been invented to square with an obscure prophecy.

Modern readers are fascinated by the psychological reasons that motivated Judas to betray Jesus, and many possibilities have been suggested. Suffice it to say that these suggestions are all highly speculative and have no basis whatever in the texts.

It is possible however to offer some explanation as to why the Sanhedrin needed the services of Judas in order to arrest Jesus. The answer lies in Mark 14:2=Matt. 26:5, where the phrase "not during the feast" should properly be translated "not in the presence of the crowd gathered for the feast." The religious authorities did not want to arrest Jesus in public for they wanted to avoid a demonstration or an uprising in protest. Judas, fortunately for the Sanhedrin, knew where Jesus would be found at night and so was able to lead the temple police to the right spot.

Matthew again follows Mark closely in his account of the preparation for the Passover. But he changes the words in which Jesus instructs the two disciples. Instead of having Jesus predict that they will find a man carrying water in a jar, Matthew simply says they will find "a certain person." In other words, the meeting takes place by prearrangement on Jesus' part rather than by supernatural insight.

Matthew deletes the further details of what the two disciples will find in the upper room and substitutes a solemn message that they are to deliver to the man after the rendezvous: "My time is at hand." This phrase has an almost Johannine ring about it. Jesus' death is set in a framework of apocalyptic inevitability.

Whereas Mark says that Jesus came with the twelve (Mark 14:17), Matthew says that Jesus "sat at table with the twelve," for the two disciples were already there! The figure of Judas at the table stands out more clearly. Judas, like Jesus' enemies elsewhere in the Gospel of Matthew, addresses Jesus as Rabbi, whereas the others call him Kyrie (Lord). It is not just any one of the disciples who is to betray Jesus but a specific disciple, the one who has already signified his identity by dipping his hand into the dish. Judas asks whether Jesus has singled him out and Jesus replies, "You have said so," meaning "You have condemned yourself out of your own mouth."

All of these changes bring out a special feature of Matthew's redaction of the Passion narrative—one which he shares with John. Jesus is always master of the situation. It is he who sets events in motion. And he does so in full knowledge that he is thereby carrying out God's plan in salvation history.

Matthew, by his subtle alterations to his Markan source, supports Paul's interpretation of the cross as at once a human act of obedience on the part of Jesus and also an act of God himself. But it is to Paul that we have to go to discover the salvific consequences of that double act. We would therefore suggest that if the preacher wishes to preach a doctrinal sermon, she or he take the epistle reading as the text, simply using the Gospel reading to confirm the duality of the cross as an act of human obedience and of God's salvation. If however the preacher wishes to concentrate on the Gospel text he or she could take Judas's question, "Is it I, Master?" and use it as a call to self-examination before Holy Communion. As the disciples prepared the Supper, so we must prepare ourselves for the Holy Communion on Maundy Thursday, Good Friday, or Easter Day.

Maundy Thursday

Lutheran	Roman Catholic	Episcopal	Pres/UCC/Chr	Meth/COCU
Exod. 24:3–11	Exod. 12:1–8, 11–14	Exod. 12:1–14a	Deut. 16:1–8	Exod. 24:3–11 or Deut. 16:1–8
1 Cor. 10:16–17 (18–21)	1 Cor. 11:23–26	1 Cor. 11:23–26 (27–32)	Rev. 1:4–8	1 Cor. 10:16–21
Mark 14:12–26	John 13:1–15	John 13:1–15 or Luke 22:14–30	Matt. 26:17–30	Mark 14:12–26 or John 13:1–17, 34

This day, liturgically, has a number of different associations. First, as the name of the day itself indicates, it is the day of the foot washing at which Jesus gave the disciples a "new commandment" that they love one another. The Latin word *commandment (mandatum)* is the source of the name *Maundy*. This was also the day when penitents who had been placed under discipline during the Lenten season were restored to full fellowship in the eucharistic community in time for Easter. The bishop on this day blessed the holy oils for use during the ensuing year at the so-called chrism mass. More recently, in the Roman Catholic church, it has become the day when priests renew their priestly vows. Finally, there is the commemoration of the institution of the Lord's Supper. The readings we follow here are focused upon this event to the exclusion of all other associations of Maundy Thursday.

There is indeed a wisdom in this concentration. A popular opinion among Protestants is that the Lord's Supper, or Eucharist, is celebrated in memory of or as a commemoration of the Last Supper. This is a mistaken notion. The Lord's Supper, or Eucharist, is a commemoration of the whole saving work of Christ, with special focus on his death: "As often as you eat this bread and drink the cup, you proclaim the Lord's death until he comes." Or, as the traditional anamnesis paragraph in the Great Eucharistic Prayer puts it, we have in remembrance "his blessed passion and precious death, his mighty resurrection and glorious ascension." The institution of the Holy Supper is commemorated specifically only on this day.

A further point to be borne in mind about this celebration of the institution of the Holy Communion and about Maundy Thursday itself is that it is not an isolated commemoration in itself but is part of what the Roman Catholics call the paschal mystery. Originally, and indeed right up to the fourth century, the paschal mystery was celebrated as a single, unitary feast. More important theologically, it was celebrated not as a commemoration of historical events but as a proclamation and participation in an eschatological event. It was not until after the Constantinian revolution, when the church first became recognized and later became the official religion of the Roman Empire, that it acquired a new sense of its historical past and turned from eschatological celebration to historical commemoration. Thus Cyril of Jerusalem even staged an Upper Room commemoration of the Last Supper on the Thursday before Easter, with a procession along the Via Dolorosa to the hill of Calvary on Good Friday and then a service at the site of the sepulcher on Easter Sunday morning. Historical commemoration had replaced eschatological celebration and the original unitary feast was thus split into its component parts. But Maundy Thursday, Good Friday, and Easter Day belong together and should be celebrated as an integrated whole. The three days are meant to be a complete liturgical experience, and Christians should not regard themselves as free to choose which day they like to attend services and think that thereby they are performing their Easter duty. Second, we have to try and recover a sense of eschatological celebration and of participation in the paschal mystery. That is the whole purpose of these three days: our passing through the transition from death to life, from darkness to light, from sin to righteousness.

FIRST LESSON: EXODUS 24:3–11

This pericope recounts the ceremony of the covenant ratification at Mount Sinai. It occurs immediately after Moses descends from the mountaintop where he received the Decalogue.

As it stands, our reading falls into two parts, the first being the Elohist account (vv. 3–8) and the second, the Yahwist (vv. 9–11). We will comment on each of them in turn and then pick out what is of permanent significance for Christian faith.

The Elohist account is the more democratic of the two versions. Here the whole people are directly involved. The people vocally assent to the law: "All the words (that is, the Decalogue) which the Lord has spoken we will do" (v. 3). The pillars of course represent the twelve tribes. The blood of burnt offerings and peace offerings is thrown, half of it against the altar (v. 6) and half upon the people. Moses interprets his action with the words: "Behold the blood of the covenant which the Lord has made with you" (v. 8). This double sprinkling upon the altar (representing Yahweh) and on the people brings the people into the closest possible participation in the covenant.

The Yahwist account is more aristocratic. Here only the elders participate as representatives of the whole people. They go up the mountain apart from the people, whereas in the Elohist version the ceremony took place at the foot of the mountain (v. 4) in the immediate presence of the people. The party having ascended the mountain is granted a vision of Yahweh: "They saw the God of Israel" (v. 10). But this can hardly mean a direct vision. For even Moses later was only allowed to see Yahweh from the back (Exod. 33:17–23) and Isaiah only saw his "glory," the outward manifestation of his presence. So it is here; they see only the pavement of sapphire beneath Yahweh's feet, that is the firmament of heaven. Whereas the first version of the covenant ratification culminated with the sprinkling of the blood upon the people, this version reaches its climax in a common meal or, as the Yahwist puts it concisely, "they ate and drank." It is a covenant meal, which serves the same purpose as the sprinkling of the blood. It brings the people through their representatives into the closest possible association with the covenant.

It is impossible to get a completely adequate translation and English equivalent for the word translated *covenant*. The Hebrew word *berith* is derived from the oriental practice in which defeated enemies were forced to accept terms of peace dictated by a conquering potentate. *Covenant* suggests two equal parties. In the case of the covenant between Yahweh and his people, the initiative rests entirely on the side of Yahweh: the people respond by accepting Yahweh's terms, and Yahweh makes them participators in the covenant through a quasi-sacramental rite.

True, there are examples in the Old Testament of covenants between equal parties, especially between individuals, such as between Jonathan and David (1 Sam. 20:8). But such individual pacts are different from the great covenants between Yahweh and Israel which constituted them his people. This has to be remembered when the word *covenant* is taken up into the New Testament. The covenant inaugurated by Christ's death is on a par with the greatest theological covenants of the Old Testament, in that the initiative lies wholly on the side of God although the people have to respond. We do not make such covenants with God.

The older word *Testament,* on the other hand, is too one-sided. Although the Epistle to the Hebrews (9:16, 17) picks up this sense of the word *diathēkē* to score a point, arguing that the death of the testator is necessary to inaugurate a will, it is not suitable in other contexts, for there has to be a prior response or acceptance from the other party. As our present reading indicates, there had to be participation and a communion between the two parties, either through the sprinkling of sacrificial blood or through a communion meal.

The word over the cup at the Last Supper refers in all versions of the tradition to a covenant. In fact, as we have already argued, there can be little doubt that Jesus himself actually did speak of a covenant at the Last Supper (Matt. 26:28) and suggested his death was somehow to inaugurate it. In the Markan version, whether it represents the actual form of the saying spoken by Jesus or not, there is a clear allusion to Exodus 24:8, "This is my blood-of-the-covenant." Some early Christian community, if it was not Jesus himself, saw in the Exodus ratification ceremony an analogy to the Christian Eucharist. In point of fact, Christian interpretation takes up elements from both versions of the story. The words we have just quoted come from the Elohist version, in which the blood is sprinkled upon the people, but the actual communion rite accompanying the words is one of eating and drinking as in the Yahwist version. On the whole, however, it would seem that the Elohist version provided imagery for Christian baptism rather than for the Eucharist, for 1 Peter speaks of the "sprinkling with his blood" in a context which is full of baptismal allusions (1 Pet. 1:2). Thus it may be said that the Elohist account provides background for the inauguration of the covenant for Christians in baptism and the Yahwist account background for the renewal of the covenant in the Eucharist.

The two types of sacrifice, burnt offering and peace offering, are important for the Christian interpretation of the death of Christ and of the Eucharist. As the burnt offering is a sacrifice of the whole victim, so Christ's sacrifice is an act of total self-surrender, in perfect obedience (for example, Phil. 2:8). But in the Eucharist we too are caught up into his sacrifice. We offer "ourselves, our souls and bodies" as a "reasonable, holy and living sacrifice." We are enclosed in his sacrifice, just as the children of Israel were enclosed in the covenant sacrifice as the blood was sprinkled upon them and as they ate and drank at the covenant meal.

The peace offering, too, is fulfilled in Christ. He is our peace, and in the Communion we participate in that peace. In that meal we are reconciled to God and thus receive the peace of God, which passes all understanding.

The preacher may well choose today to preach a sermon on the Lord's Supper entirely from this Exodus reading. Interpreted typologically, it provides abundant material on the topic of the Eucharist: covenant meal, remembrance of covenant sacrifice, burnt offering, peace offering, communion in the covenant, communion in Christ's sacrifice, self-oblation in his self-oblation. Or the preacher may prefer to bring out some of these themes incidentally when interpreting the New Testament readings, especially, for example, the cup word in the Markan account of the institution.

SECOND LESSON: 1 CORINTHIANS 10:16–21

If there had not been troubles in Corinth necessitating a discussion of issues concerning the celebration of the Lord's Supper, we would have no references whatever to the Eucharist in Paul's letters, and no doubt some clever professor would have asserted that the Eucharist was unknown in the Pauline churches! Fortunately for us, there were troubles at Corinth, and Paul had to refer several times to the Lord's Supper in 1 Corinthians. In our present context the reference is occasioned by the participation of some of the "enlightened" Corinthians in pagan sacrificial meals. They thought that having been initiated into *gnosis* by Christ in baptism they knew that pagan deities have no reality and therefore the requirements of social conformity could be met without any harm to themselves or anyone else. Paul has to admonish his converts to "shun the worship of idols." Participation in the Holy Communion excludes participation in the cup of demons. Thus quite incidentally and in passing Paul gives us some of the most important doctrinal statements about the Eucharist to be found in the New Testament.

In order to make his point that the Corinthians should refrain from partaking in pagan meals, Paul begins by quoting what is almost certainly a traditional formula (v. 16). Perhaps the formula was an affirmative statement. In that case Paul would have thrown it into the interrogative form because he wishes to remind the Corinthians of a tradition they already knew. It is most probable, too, that in the pre-Pauline formula the bread and cup sayings were in the reverse order. Paul has shifted the order around because he wished to comment at length on the saying about the bread, thus ignoring the saying about the cup. In 11:24–25 he shows quite clearly that he and his churches performed the rite in the usual order of bread and cup. Paul is not quoting the tradition for its own sake as a piece of liturgical catechesis but is engaged in theological argument.

The term "cup of blessing" is a technical term in Judaism, denoting the final cup at the Jewish passover meal. It is the cup over which there is said the blessing: "Blessed art thou, O Lord our God, who givest us the fruit of the vine." Note that in Hebrew custom it is not the cup which is blessed, but Yahweh, in thanksgiving for the cup. The additional phrase, "which we bless" with *cup* as its object is Hellenistic rather than Jewish. To bless or to give thanks is the same thing. The word translated *participation* (RSV margin *communion*) is charged with profound theological meaning. The Eucharist constitutes an indwelling: we in Christ and Christ in us. It sets up something more than an I-thou relationship in continued separation. Participation in his body and blood means participation in him as the one who died a sacrificial death. Body and blood are not substances or things but person and event, Christ in his self-giving unto death. He is personally present in the event of his sacrificial death, and we are drawn into his sacrifice through eating the bread and drinking the cup. Note that it is "we" who break the bread just as it is "we" who bless the cup. The eucharistic president (for someone has to preside and do it) does not act for himself or do on behalf of others what they cannot do for themselves, but rather he acts as their representative. The Eucharist is a corporate act of the whole church.

Paul's comment in v. 17 is directly related to the context of this discussion. Participation in the common loaf constitutes the communicants as the (ecclesial) body of Christ because through the one loaf they participate in his sacramental body. (Note that individual wafers or separate cubes of bread obscure the meaning of the rite as interpreted by Paul just as much as individual communion cups do). The purpose and result of Holy Communion or Holy Participation is not merely the conveyance of grace to the individual: it constitutes or rather renews the gathered assembly as the ecclesial body of Christ.

What has this argument to do with the avoidance of pagan rites? Surely it must be that whether or not the idols or the demons are real in those other rites, they have the same corporate effect as participation in the Lord's Supper. They make the participants members of the idols or demons and also members of an idolatrous community. Participation in Christ and the consequent participation in his ecclesial body therefore rule out participation in pagan feasts. The two are mutually exclusive.

The rest of the paragraph reinforces this exclusiveness. It provides analogies for the purpose of illustration, not proofs. We cannot argue from these verses that the Lord's Supper is a sacrificial meal in the sense that the Jewish or pagan cultic meals were sacrificial meals. The Eucharist is not a rite in which a new sacrifice is repeatedly offered, but one in which there is a remembrance of a once-for-all sacrifice and a participation in its salvific consequences. Thus among cultic rites the Eucharist is sui generis. If we call it a sacrifice and the table of the Lord an altar, we do so in quite a different sense from the pagan or Jewish usages.

It is clear that the Pauline comment on the traditional formula cited in verse 17 calls for particular emphasis on the corporate nature of the Lord's Supper. This has long been obscured in the Christian West, both among Catholics and Protestants. The Roman Catholic abuse—now rectified since the liturgical changes following Vatican II—was that the faithful were occupied in their individual devotions on their knees (with their rosaries or little books of devotions) while the essential actions of the Mass were performed by the sacred ministers at the altar. Protestantism likewise has all too often interpreted the Lord's Supper merely as an occasion when the individual received the forgiveness of sins or grace for amendment of life, and growth in individual sanctity—what Bishop John A. T. Robinson once called the "tanking up" view of Holy Communion. Of course the Eucharist *is* all that. But these things are incidental byproducts. The really important effect of it, according to Paul, is that it is an action of the whole body that reconstitutes the whole body to be what it is, the body of Christ. This is the emphasis for which our text calls, and the emphasis that the preacher may well want to put across today. But note that it is not corporateness for its own sake. *Koinonia* is not jolly, back-slapping togetherness. It is not human fellowship—a word which should be put into cold storage for a while. It is participation in the redemptive event of the paschal mystery. It is by partaking of that mystery that we become or are renewed as the body of Christ. As Bishop Lord Ramsey, the former Archbishop of Canterbury, has said, the point is not that the church is the *body* of Christ, but rather that it is the body of *Christ*.

Alternatively the preacher may wish to emphasize the traditional formula which Paul quotes, rather than the Apostle's editorial comments. In that case he or she will wish to expound the doctrine of the real presence. This has been a very divisive issue among Christians in the past. We have excommunicated one another, burnt one another at the stake, entered into schism, hurled anathemas at each other, and everything else besides. Today there appears to be a real convergence in this matter. This is signalized by the Dutch Catholic use of the word *transignification,* a concept which comes close to the high Reformed doctrine. The bread and wine in the eucharistic rite become the effective signs or symbols of Christ's body and blood, conveying what they symbolize. A good illustration of this is the dollar bill. When I give someone a dollar bill, the piece of paper does not become itself a gold coin of that amount (the popular Roman view before Vatican II, condemned by the Reformers). Nor does it merely say that you already have a coin of that amount in your pocket (the view commonly attributed to Zwingli). It actually conveys to you that value. It is to *all intents and purposes* a gold coin of that value, though out of the context of its use it is still just a piece of paper. It derives that meaning from the promise of the Federal Reserve Board: "This note is legal tender for all debts, public and private." These words have a similar power and effect as, in another context, the words: "This is my body" and "This is my blood."

GOSPEL: MARK 14:12–26

Of the various alternative Gospel readings for this day we have, according to the principles of this commentary, selected the Lutheran (which also happens to be the Methodist/COCU alternative) reading for this day. It has two disadvantages, however. It was part of the longer reading already used on Sunday, and it also overlaps in content with the reading from Matthew, which was read in most lectionaries and was selected for comment above. Because of these duplications we shall ignore in our comments here the sections covering the preparations for the Supper and the unmasking of Judas, and concentrate on the institution of the Eucharist.

Commentators from a Lutheran or Reformed background often define this pericope as a liturgy or at least as material to be used in liturgy. This is due to a late medieval misunderstanding of the nature of the eucharistic rite, a misunderstanding which is fortunately being corrected in most recent revisions. For it was a late medieval idea that the essential core of the eucharistic consecration was the recitation of the words of institution. This idea survives in the second form of consecration provided in the *Lutheran Book of Worship,* but its provision there can only be regarded as a concession to liturgical conservatism and hopefully will fall into disuse. Rather, the institution pericope should be regarded as a liturgical *catechesis,* or agenda. It describes what you have to do in order to carry out the rite. To do the Eucharist it is necessary to

1. Take bread
2. Say the blessing
3. Break the bread
4. Give or distribute the bread, accompanying the distribution with the words of promise that this bread is the Lord's body
5. (Implied; the communicants) eat the bread
6. Take a cup (of wine) according to Jewish ritual
7. Give thanks
8. Give the cup
9. (The Communicants) receive the cup.

Mark's description follows the usage that originally obtained when the bread and the cup were separated by an intervening meal (see "after supper," 1 Cor. 11:25). When the meal was omitted and the bread and cup rites were brought together, actions 1 and 2 were combined with 6 and 7, so as to produce a rite like this:

1. Take bread and wine
2. Say the blessing over/give thanks over the bread and wine
3. Break the bread
4. Distribute and eat the bread (with words of distribution)
5. Distribute and drink from the cup (with words of distribution).

Note that the words "This is my body" and "This is my blood" belong properly to the distribution, not to the consecration, which takes the form of a blessing (of the name of God) or thanksgiving (to God), according to Jewish custom. Of course, it became customary also to include the words of institution within the Great Thanksgiving, but they should be interpreted, not as consecratory, but as part of the thanksgiving for what the Lord has instituted and promised. They could conceivably be omitted, as was the case in the *Didache* (c. 100) and some other early liturgies, though few churches today omit them. Sometimes they appear separately from the thanksgiving, as in the current Presbyterian rite. There they function as a charter narrative.

The words, then, are not rightly characterized as words of consecration: they are words that interpret what is being eaten. That is to say, when we eat this bread and drink this cup we become in Paul's language partakers of this body and blood, as we explained in our comments on the epistle reading: that is, we partake, not in things, but in the saving event in which Jesus was the actor and in its saving consequences. Consecration is effected by the thanksgiving, or blessing (not of the bread and the cup, but of the name of God in thanksgiving). By *consecration* we do not mean that the bread and wine are changed into something else but that their use is diverted from ordinary use to a sacramental use. The eating and drinking of these particular elements thus set apart, is to be the means of *koinonia* in Christ's body and blood or saving act.

In addition to the words of distribution, Mark includes a saying technically known as the *eschatological prospect* (Mark 14:25): "Truly I say to you, I shall not drink again of the fruit of the vine until that day when I drink it new in the Kingdom of God." In the Lukan version of the Supper a similar saying *precedes* the action with the bread and wine and in part accompanies the first cup. (Luke has two cups, the first one probably corresponding to an extra cup used in Christian Passover celebrations in the Lukan community; Mark has the form which was used on ordinary occasions throughout the year.) The eschatological prospect survives in the Pauline account only in a somewhat attenuated form in the statement that whenever we eat the bread and drink the cup we show forth the Lord's death "until he comes." But it did not die out completely. It is strongly emphasized in the *Didache* in the prayer:

As grain once scattered on the hillsides
was in this broken bread made one,
So from all lands thy Church be gathered
into thy kingdom by thy Son.
(The Episcopal Hymnal 1940, #195)

Something of the same notion survives in the great eucharistic hymns of St. Thomas Aquinas, as for instance:

Jesus, whom now veiled, I by faith descry
What my soul doth long for, do not, Lord, deny,
That, thy face unveiled, I at last may see,
With the blissful vision blest, my God of thee.
(The Episcopal Hymnal 1940, #204).

Surprisingly, the eschatological note is given much stronger expression in the hymn of a nineteenth century Evangelical, Horatius Bonar:

Feast after feast thus comes and passes by,
Yet, passing, points to the glad feast above,
Giving us a foretaste of the festal joy,
The Lord's eternal feast of bliss and love.
(The Episcopal Hymnal 1940, #206)

By and large however in the Western tradition this eschatological emphasis has faded until recently. This is the reason for the excessively penitential and Calvary-centered character of much of Protestant eucharistic practice. Recent liturgical renewal has tried to recover some of the eschatological emphasis, as in the congregational response:

Christ has died.
Christ has risen.
Christ will come again.

Or in another form of response:

We remember his death,
We proclaim his resurrection,
We await his coming in glory.

The simple white alb is therefore being used more and more at the Lord's table in both Catholic and Protestant celebrations because it is an eschatological vestment par excellence. The saints in heaven are described in Revelation (7:9) as wearing the white robes of victory. They have made their robes white in the blood of the lamb and are able to participate in the Supper of the Lamb.

The Markan account of the Last Supper concludes with the singing of a hymn. This has been frequently identified with the second group of Hallel psalms (Psalms 114—118) of the Jewish Passover liturgy. More likely, however, it represents the custom of the Markan church on ordinary occasions. We read this account, not primarily as a description of what happened at the Last Supper, but as a description of the liturgy of Mark's church.

After the hymn Jesus and his disciples go out into the Mount of Olives. This has an important bearing on the Maundy Thursday celebration. It is a festal occasion, celebrating the institution of the Eucharist, in a week which is otherwise solemn and penitential. But it is important that the rejoicing should close in a way that expresses the going out of the disciples into the Garden of Gethsemane. Increasingly this is done by removing all candles and other ornaments from the church before the people leave, stripping the altar bare, and letting the congregation leave in silence and in darkness. The effect is very powerful. The "brief bright hour" of festivity is over. We now resume the solemn mood of following our Lord to his agony, his trial, and the cross. At all events, we should not come out of church that evening in a festal mood as a fully lighted and decorated church and the strains of a triumphant postlude on the organ would tend to create.

If the preacher wants to concentrate on eucharistic doctrine he or she would probably preach upon the epistle reading. If he wants to speak about the Eucharist as an action or rite, he would preach upon the Gospel reading. Mark gives us an opportunity in the eschatological prospect to emphasize the eschatological joy of the Eucharist, and where the Lord's Supper has been associated with excessive penitential gloom, a sermon on the eschatological prospect might help to redress the balance. There may be other matters in our mode of celebration which require reform in the light of Scripture, such as the recovery of the Great Thanksgiving, the proper breaking of the one loaf, and the like. Or maybe we have a renewed liturgy already, but our congregation does not understand the point of it all. In that case the Markan account of the Last Supper may provide a rationale for some of the new features of the rite that are not properly appreciated.

Good Friday

Lutheran	Roman Catholic	Episcopal	Pres/UCC/Chr	Meth/COCU
Isa. 52:13—53:12 or Hos. 6:1-6	Isa. 52:13—53:12	Isa. 52:13—53:12 or Gen. 22:1-18 or Wisd. 2:1, 12-24	Lam. 1:7-12	Isa. 52:13—53:12
Heb. 4:14-16; 5:7-9	Heb. 4:14-16; 5:7-9	Heb. 10:1-25	Heb. 10:4-18	Heb. 4:14-16; 5:7-9 or Heb. 10:1-25
John 18:1—19:42 or John 19:17-30	John 18:1—19:42	John (18:1-40) 19:1-37	Luke 23:33-46	John 18:1—19:42 or Luke 23:33-46

In liturgical preaching—that is, preaching that is set in context of the liturgy and that seeks to clarify and support the liturgical action—it is important to be aware of precisely what that liturgical setting is. Good Friday is a particular occasion in point, for the Service of the Word has a unique character on this day.

This is a description of the Good Friday liturgy in the *Book of Common Prayer,* 1979: The service begins in silence with the church stripped bare of ornament. After silent prayer the Service of the Word is conducted in the usual manner, though it differs in the long reading of the Passion according to John. The Passion may be read dramatically, specific roles being assigned to different persons and the congregation taking the part of the crowd.

After the sermon comes the solemn intercession that follows the primitive pattern of such prayer, which elsewhere has fallen into disuse:

1. Subjects for intercession are announced by a deacon or other appointed person.
2. The people pray individually in silence.
3. Their prayers are summed up in a collect said by the presiding minister.

This prayer is a cooperative action of minister and people, not a clerical monologue. Then a large wooden cross may be brought into the church and placed in the sight of the people while appropriate devotions follow, including the familiar *Salvator mundi:*

O Savior of the world
who by thy cross and precious blood hast redeemed us:
Save us and help us we humbly beseech thee O Lord

Traditionally a very moving part of these devotions was the so-called reproaches. In these, the mighty acts God has done in history for his people are recited, and the people reproached for their rejection and crucifixion of Jesus. The language of the reproaches is largely taken from Jeremiah, but every Good Friday preacher must avoid anything that could possibly be construed as anti-Semitism. Great sensitivity is required in this matter, especially when dealing with the Passion narratives of Matthew and John.

The Good Friday service may then conclude with the administration of the Holy Communion. Of all days in the year, this day seems particularly appropriate for showing the Lord's death until he comes.

If this practice is followed, then we may have three different celebrations of Holy Communion over Maundy Thursday, Good Friday, and Easter Day. Each has its own different parts of the paschal mystery. It is the preacher's task each day to aid the congregation in its participation in each aspect of this mystery.

SECOND LESSON:
HEBREWS 4:14–16; 5:7–9

Like the composer of a symphony, the author of Hebrews enunciates his theme, Christ the High Priest, several times before he develops it. This development will not come until chapter 7. The first enunciation of the theme came at Heb. 2:17; the second, at Heb. 3:1; the third, at 4:14; the fourth, at 5:5–6. The reasons for these successive enunciations of the theme are twofold. First, the writer wishes to clear away any possible objection to applying the title "High Priest" to Jesus and to insist that in spite of these objections he has all the important qualifications for high priesthood.

After all it was by no means obvious to any first century person brought up on the Old Testament and in Judaism that Christ could legitimately be called a high priest at all. The problem was that he was not of Levitical descent. This is the point of the citation from Psalm 110:4 (Heb. 5:6 and the like). This verse shows that the Old Testament recognized another high priesthood, one after the order of Melchizedek, that is, an eschatological high priesthood that was destined to replace the Levitical or Aaronic. So Jesus' descent from Judah (Heb. 7:14) does not disqualify him from being a high priest. And he preeminently holds all the personal qualifications. He was human, one of us. He suffered and was tempted and is therefore able to help us when we are tempted (Heb. 2:14–18). He was faithful to his commission (3:2–6). He is able to sympathize with our weaknesses and, once again, has known what temptation is (4:15). He is chosen from among human beings and appointed to act on their behalf in relation to God—his function is a Godward one. He offers to God sacrifice for sin (5:1), appears in the presence of God for us, and makes intercession for us (Heb. 7:25; 9:24). He is not self-appointed but appointed by God (Heb. 5:4–5). This took place at his exaltation and enthronement, as the citation of Ps. 2:7 at Heb. 5:5 shows.

The second reason for this repeated enunciation of the theme is that the author of Hebrews keeps getting sidetracked by the need to exhort his readers. In fact exhortation was the overall purpose of his work, which he calls, not a letter, but a "word of exhortation" (Heb. 13:22). Even the great doctrinal section that runs from 7:1 through 10:18 is not an exposition of doctrine for doctrine's sake but is subservient to the exhortation that begins at 10:19 and runs through chapter 12.

There is not very much evidence to suggest that the addressees were running into doctrinal heresy. Rather, their situation was that they had been Christians for a long time and were beginning to suffer from boredom. The author sees a real parallel between their situation and what happened to the Israelites in the wilderness between Egypt and the promised land. In the wilderness God had provided for his people a priesthood, a tent of his presence, and cultic sacrifices (that is what, according to the author of Hebrews, the law was all about—not about moral commands). Israel however neglected and disobeyed that law. Now that God has provided a perfect high priest, sanctuary, sacrifices, and the like for his eschatological people as they "wander between the times," that is, between the first and second comings of Christ, how much more should they be careful not to neglect what God has provided for them. For what God has provided in his new, great high priest is final. Neglect that great salvation, and there is no chance of working one's passage back again. In that case, he says, you've had it.

We have then, says our author in the present pericope (4:14), a great high priest. This "have" is the indicative of the Christian life. But the

indicative implies an imperative: we must hold fast to "our confession," not let it slip away, as the addressees of the author were doing in
their increasing boredom with Christian faith and life. Does this mean
that the confession contained an affirmation that Jesus was our High
Priest? Probably not, despite this verse and the earlier reference in
Hebrews 3:1 to Jesus as the High Priest of our confession. The
Christian confession was always in terms of Jesus as Christ (Messiah),
Lord, and Son of God. The doctrine of his high priesthood belongs,
not to the primary confession, but to secondary theological exposition. But as is shown in Hebrews 5:5–6, the passage omitted from our
pericope, the doctrine is closely connected with and arises out of the
primary confession of Jesus as the Son of God. He who said, "Thou
art my Son, today have I begotten thee," said also in another psalm,
"Thou are a priest for ever, after the order of Melchizedek." It is
because Jesus is confessed as Son of God and installed as such at his
resurrection that we can also say that he is our great High Priest. That
is why in v. 14 the author inserts parenthetically after "Jesus" the title
Son of God. The reason for this becomes clear at 5:5–6. The title High
Priest is also connected with the title Lord *(Kyrios),* for in v. 1 of
Psalm 110 we read that the messianic king who is in verse 4 to be
designated priest after the order of Melchizedek, is first addressed by
the psalmist as "my Lord." Thus we see that the High Priest belongs
not to the primary confession, but develops from the primary confession of Jesus as being—from his resurrection—Christ, Lord, and Son
of God. He is a great high priest, or as we would say, he is the
eschatological High Priest, the one who perfects all that the Levitical
high priest could not. He has "passed through" the heavens, a description of Jesus' ascension or exaltation (the author, as we saw in our
comments for the epistle reading on Monday, almost invariably thinks
in terms of exaltation or ascension, rather than of resurrection). In an
almost Johannine way, he thinks of the death of Jesus as the moment
in which he passes through the veil of his flesh and enters into the
presence of God. This omission of any reference to the resurrection
need not surprise us. Resurrection is only one of the linguistic models
employed in the New Testament to speak of the vindication of Jesus
out of death. Exaltation is another model for speaking about the same
thing. Nor should we be surprised that a reading for Good Friday
should speak of Christ's exaltation. We are engaged today not in the
business of historical commemoration, but in participation in the total

paschal mystery. The primary emphasis today is of course on its cross-side, but the reading properly reminds us of the other side also.

The word for *passed through (dialēluthota)* is a powerful expression. It means *striding through victoriously*. The contrast with the picture in the second paragraph of our pericope is striking, almost paradoxical. The plural *heavens* may reflect Hebrew usage, or it may be that the author accepts the apocalyptic view that there were three (cf. 2 Cor. 12:2) or seven heavens.

The connecting word *for* in v. 15 states why we have every reason to hold fast to our confession of Jesus as Son of God and therefore as our High Priest. This reason is stated first negatively and then positively. Negatively, he is not unable (as he would be if he were a purely heavenly figure) to sympathize with our weaknesses. Positively, Jesus has been through our temptations yet is without sin. The author, as he shows clearly in the second paragraph of our pericope, is not thinking of the Temptation story at the beginning of Jesus' ministry but of the agony in the Garden of Gethsemane. He was tempted but "without sin." This last phrase is not the result of empirical assessment, as though the author counted up everything Jesus had done in his life and found that he had never committed a single sin. Rather, since he is thinking of Gethsemane, it means that Jesus utterly and completely accepted his Father's will for him and went obediently to the cross. "Not my will, but thine, be done." How was he tempted? He wanted to be saved from that gruesome death. In his human weakness he shrank from it and uttered loud cries with tears: "Abba, Father, all things are possible to thee; remove this cup from me" (Mark 14:36). If the preacher wishes to be helped in bringing home to his congregation what a terrible death crucifixion was, he should read a book like Martin Hengel's *Crucifixion*. This will help him to present graphically to his congregation why Jesus contemplated the prospect with such terror. The mention of "tears" as well as loud cries suggests that the author of Hebrews was familiar with the longer Lukan form of the Gethsemane story.

Hebrews 4:16, which is part of our reading, would seem to come more logically after 5:10, for then the whole doctrinal section (the indicative) would be uninterrupted, and the pericope would conclude with the imperative which arises out of the doctrine: "Let us draw near." The words *draw near* are cultic words, meaning draw near to worship. This very expression occurs in the invitation to Communion in the old *Book of Common Prayer* and in the Methodist rite: "Draw near with faith and take this Holy Sacrament to your comfort." If the Holy Communion is to be administered in this service, an exposition of this verse would make an admirable climax to a sermon on this reading from Hebrews. The preacher would then expound how Jesus, our great High Priest, can sympathize with us in our temptations and expound the passion as revealed in the Gethsemane prayer as Jesus' last temptation.

GOSPEL: JOHN 18:1—19:42

There was probably in existence a pre-gospel Passion narrative from which the various passions in the Gospels (except Matthew, which seems to have been simply a reediting of Mark) were derived. John however also has a special tradition that should not be dismissed as historically worthless. Where he derived this from cannot be known with certainty. One is tempted to suppose that it comes from the eyewitness mentioned in John 19:35. This witness is usually identified with the beloved disciple. There are several references to an unnamed disciple in the Passion and Resurrection narratives. There is first the disciple whom Jesus loved. He is mentioned as present at the Last Supper (John 13:23) where he overhears the unmasking of Judas. He is at the foot of the cross where he receives the mother of Jesus into his care and takes her to his own home (19:25–27). He runs with Peter to check out the grave on Easter Sunday morning (20:3–10), and in the appended chapter 21 he is present at the resurrection appearance by the Lake of Galilee (21:20–23). Then there is "another disciple" who is mentioned as securing Peter's entry into the High Priest's court (18:15). If these all refer to the same person, we have here a witness who was present over the whole course of events from the Last Supper to the end of the story, and we can link him with some of the traditions which are peculiar to the Johannine Passion narrative over and above the common passion tradition. These pieces of information would include such local topographical knowledge as the brook Kidron, the pavement Gabbatha, and the fact that Jesus was buried in a garden. There are also a number of other pieces of factual information that are unique to the Fourth Gospel and that sometimes allow us plausibly to supplement or correct the other gospels. We have already mentioned the dating of the Last Supper on the eve of the Passover. That obviously affects, too, the dating of Jesus' trial and execution. It is much more plausible to think that all of this took place on the day *before* the feast, which would then have begun at sundown after Jesus had died. At Jesus' arrest not only the temple police but also a detachment of Roman legionaries took part. This fact (though the term "band" suggests an implausibly large figure, a thousand men) is quite possibly historical if we suppose that the chief priests and the Roman prefect were already collaborating to get rid of Jesus. John's statement that after he was arrested Jesus was first taken, not to the Sanhedrin as in Mark, but for a private investigation before Annas, is again quite possible. For Josephus, the Jewish historian, indicates that Annas, although deposed many years since, still remained the real power behind the throne during the high priesthood of his son-in-law Caiaphas. It is also unlikely that the whole Sanhedrin would have met late at night and more much plausible that it assembled early enough in the morning to complete the proceedings before the opening of Pilate's court. John's Gospel is also quite convincing on what happened before Annas questioned Jesus about his disciples and his teaching. It looks as though the intention was to get Jesus to incriminate himself as a messianic pretender. Quite plausibly, too, Jesus demands that proper legal procedures be followed and that proper witnesses should be produced.

Some of the uniquely Johannine details of Pilate's trial of Jesus are also quite plausible—for instance, the refusal of the religious authorities to enter Pilate's court lest they defile themselves for the feast and Pilate's consequent going in and out of the court to the street outside.

More problematical is the claim that Mary the mother of Jesus was present at the crucifixion. It is not surprising that Mark omits this, for he has a negative attitude toward Jesus' family (Mark 3:21, 31–35). But Luke has some close connection with John, especially in the Passion narrative. He also has a positive attitude toward Mary as the first Christian believer, and he tells us that Mary the mother of Jesus was present with the disciples at Jerusalem between Easter and Pentecost. It is therefore surprising that the third evangelist omits all reference to Mary at the foot of the cross if her presence there comes from a genuine gospel tradition. On the other hand, John uses the incident as a basis for a symbolic interpretation, and he does not usually invent incidents for such interpretation but applies interpretation he received from the tradition. Somewhat similar difficulties attach to the following episodes of the piercing of Jesus' side and the breaking of the legs of the other two crucified men. We simply cannot tell whether these are historical reminiscences. At most we can suppose that the evangelist received them from the tradition.

C. H. Dodd observed that John had provided all his theological interpretations in the earlier part of the Gospel, culminating in the Farewell discourses. After that the evangelist is content to let the events speak for themselves in the Passion narrative: there is no longer any discourse or dialogue. In the main this statement is true, but there are some minor exceptions. The remarkable dialogue between Jesus and Pilate on the theme of kingship (18:33–38) is similar in tone to some of the earlier discourse material. Jesus redefines kingship in a Johannine sense as witness to the truth (18:37), which means in Johannine language the bringing of revelation. Jesus throughout the Fourth Gospel is the revealer par excellence. Another Johannine reflection is found in the discussion about the source of Pilate's authority (19:10–11). This is not an abstract discussion on the nature of the state's authority but a salvation-historical assertion. Pilate has been destined to play a particular role in salvation history just as Caiaphas, the High Priest that year, was destined to pronounce the truth that it was "expedient for you that one man should die for the people" (11:51). In a similar vein, Pilate's dialogue with the chief priests after the death of Jesus about the title on the cross presents him as an instrument of salvation history: "Do not write, 'The King of the Jews' but 'This man said, I am the King of the Jews,' " To this Pilate makes the response, "What I have written, I have written" (19:19–22). Pilate is the unconscious witness to the universality of the kingship of Jesus.

As well as introducing an occasional dialogue, John also expresses his theology by a judicious use of symbolism. When Peter cuts off the ear of the High Priest's slave at the arrest (18:10), Jesus says to Peter, "Put your sword into its sheath; shall I not drink of the cup which the Father has given me?" The symbolic language of the "cup" is of course not peculiar to John. It occurs also in the synoptic version of the Gethsemane narrative (Mark 14:36) and in the saying of Jesus addressed to the two sons of Zebedee when they asked for places of honor in the kingdom (Mark 10:38–39). No doubt it occurred in the Gethsemane story of the pregospel Passion narrative and John has shifted it here. It expresses the theological truth that Jesus' death is a voluntary act of self-sacrifice. As the Johannine Christ has said in an earlier discourse, "I lay it (my life) down of my own accord" (John 10:18).

In John Jesus is always master of the situation, just as he is in Matthew, though John achieves this emphasis differently, with a series of dramatic scenes. At the arrest (John 18:2–8) Jesus presents himself voluntarily to those who come to arrest him, and when they fall back paralyzed with fear he challenges them to come forward and get on with the business. It is he who sets the passion in motion.

In the investigation before Annas (John 18:19–24) and still more in the trial before Pilate (18:28—19:16), it is really Jesus who puts his judges on trial. Pilate is shown up as a weakling whom Jesus twists round his little finger. Jesus carries his own cross to the site of his execution—no Simon of Cyrene in John (19:17). He arranges his will with his mother and the beloved disciple (19:25–27). And finally, he does not just expire: he gives back his spirit voluntarily to the Father, choosing the moment of his death and declaring in that act the salvific consequences of his death: he makes available the Spirit for his new community (John 19:30).

We have noted the common opinion that the scene of the mother of Jesus and the beloved disciple (John 19:25–27) is symbolical. But the precise nature of the symbolism is disputed. The scene has some verbal connections with the wedding at Cana of Galilee where the mother of Jesus also seems to have a symbolic role. In both scenes she is simply the mother, without mention of her name. In both scenes, too, Jesus addresses her as "woman," which though not unique to her (John 4:21), is not impolite. The Cana episode clearly points forward to the crucifixion. Jesus says there his hour has not yet come, and when he is on the cross the hour has come. The water pots at Cana were set there for the Jewish rites of purification. Now, on the cross, the supreme messianic purification is taking place: the blood of Jesus is cleansing us from our sins (1 John 1:7). It is as if what the mother of Jesus really asked for at Cana has now been granted. But is Mary's role also symbolic? And if so what is it? Many suggestions have been made. The most probable one is that in the Cana scene, Mary represents the old Israel waiting for the messianic redemption—the same role she plays in Luke's infancy narrative when she sings the Magnificat. Then, at the foot of the cross, when she is entrusted to the care of the beloved disciple, it is as though the old people of God become the new people, entrusted to the care of the apostolic witness. Thus the new people of God are continuous with the old, yet come into being through the messianic purification wrought through the cross. At the same time the apostles acquire a mother. They are not separated from the community and over against it but are themselves also products of it and dependent upon it.

This double symbolism of Mary the mother of Jesus as representing both the old community that produced the Messiah and the new community that is brought into being is also found in the enigmatic passage in Revelation 12, where the woman clothed with the sun brings forth the Messiah, thus representing the old people of God, and then suffers persecution as the new community of the Messiah.

Some have also seen here a portrayal of Mary as the new Eve (the woman whose seed is to bruise the serpent's heel [Gen. 3:15]). This is more speculative, and the connection was probably not established until the time of the second century church fathers. It is best to rest content with the symbolism of Mary as the old church and the new.

Many commentators believe that the story of the breaking of the legs has a symbolic intention. Jesus' legs were not broken, and this is stated by the evangelist to be a fulfillment of the prophecy that "Not a bone of him shall be broken" (19:36). It is not however beyond doubt that the fulfillment citation is taken from Exod. 12:46 and refers to the passover lamb. On the one hand John the Baptist had hailed Jesus as the "Lamb of God that takes away the sin of the world" (John 1:29, 36), and that greeting has often been taken as a reference to the passover lamb. Also, Jesus dies, according to the Johannine chronology, at the very moment in the afternoon before the Passover when the passover lambs are being slain. On the other hand, the citation in 19:36 could have been taken from Psalm 34:20, in which case the intention is to identify Jesus with the righteous sufferer of the Psalter. Moreover, the lamb of John the Baptist's greeting could equally be the Suffering Servant of Second Isaiah, who was led as a lamb to the slaughter (Isa. 53:7). All this makes the rather subtle identification of Jesus with the passover lamb somewhat questionable. However, in the case of the Fourth Gospel we are probably wrong if we attempt to tie the text down to one particular meaning, and the truth here, as so often, is probably that more than one meaning is intended.

In the same episode there is a further detail that invites symbolic interpretation. This is the blood and water that flowed from the side of

Jesus when it was pierced with a spear. Evidently the evangelist attaches special significance to this incident, for he calls attention to the fact that it is attested by an eyewitness, presumably once more the beloved disciple. But, once again, the precise symbolism is elusive. Water has baptismal, and blood, eucharistic associations (John 3:5; 6:53–58), and many have seen an attempt on John's part to emphasize that the two great sacraments of the Gospel have their origin on the cross. Perhaps, too, the equally enigmatic passage in 1 John 5:6 is intended to offer a clue to the meaning here. This reads: "This is he who came by water and blood, Jesus Christ, not with the water only, but with the water and the blood." The thrust of this passage is antidocetic. Does the evangelist really intend to tell us more than the simple statement that Jesus was really dead, and does the later writer of 1 John intend no more than to utilize this incident for an antidocetic argument? In our opinion the antidocetic motif in the gospel does not appear until the additions of the Johannine redactor, and was no concern of the evangelist. But the preacher may after all like to take the water and the blood as symbolic of the two sacraments, though one should be aware that in doing so one is skating on thin ice.

A favorite and highly popular type of preaching on Good Friday is to deliver a series of addresses on the so-called seven last words from the cross. This custom was a seventeenth-century Jesuit innovation, and it is ironic that long after its general demise in the Roman Catholic Church, Protestants still continue this practice. It is even more questionable when it is insisted that it take place in the three hours between 12:00 M. (noon) and 3:00 P.M., which is about the worst time to get church people together unless Good Friday is a public holiday.

There are also serious critical and theological objections to this type of Good Friday preaching. The critical objections are that it leads to false harmonization and to naive historicization. No single evangelist presents all seven of the last words. One is from Mark and Matthew, three are from Luke, and three from John. Putting them together and doing so in a traditional order which has no historical basis is simply ludicrous. Mark presents *"Eloi, Eloi, lama sabachthani?"* as Jesus' last word; Luke's version reads, "Father, into thy hands I commit my spirit;" and John's, "It is finished." These last words are alternative interpretations and not intended to be put together in a series. Mark has both the brigands revile Jesus before he dies, while Luke only has the penitent thief—a pious addition. One would like to think that Jesus really said, "Father, forgive them," but single attestation will not bear the weight of historical proof. Actually, there is some doubt about it textually. But it is probably original, for it is paralleled by Stephen's last word in Acts 7:60, as also is the word, "Father, into thy hands I commit my spirit" (see Acts 7:59). John's "I thirst" is clearly suggested by the episode of the vinegar, which belongs to the common pregospel passion. All in all, with the possible exception of the one Markan-Matthean saying, these last words are redactional, or at the very most, were pious creations of the oral tradition. This does not mean that they cannot be used as preaching texts. But they should be treated redactionally, not historically; that is to say, they should be used as clues to each evangelist's respective theology of the cross. After all, no one placed a tape recorder at the foot of the cross! Theologically, these sayings often lead the preacher astray into sentimentality. The present writer has listened to Good Friday addresses on the Johannine word, "Woman, behold your Son" which have trailed off into the virtues of family life, or one on "I thirst" which led the preacher into autobiographical reminiscences about his experiences as a desert rat in General Montgomery's army during the North African campaign of World War II—all right perhaps as illustrative material, but the address focused exclusively on the terrible character of human thirst. That is not an exegesis of the text.

One of the advantages of the lectionary, especially when used with the new liturgies, is to prevent the use of the seven last words. But it would be quite legitimate to use the three Johannine words in the lectionary *if* the preacher treats them redactionally or traditionally rather than historically.

We have already discussed the word addressed to Jesus' mother and the beloved disciple, so we will pass on to "I thirst." The context gives us little help for its interpretation beyond telling us that Jesus said it "to fulfill the scripture" (19:28). Presumably, the reference is to Psalm 69:21. Like Psalm 22, this was one of the psalms to which the early church had recourse in its Passion apologetic. Like Psalm 22, it speaks of the vindication of the righteous sufferer. In fact, the saying, "I thirst," is the theological equivalent of the Markan saying, *"Eloi, Eloi, lama sabachthani."* Here Jesus enters into the depths of the consequence of human sin. In this text, as in the Markan text, the evangelist is expressing in narrative form what Paul expressed theologically when he stated that God "made him to be sin who knew no sin so that in him we might become the righteousness of God" (2 Cor. 5:21), or again when he said that Christ became a curse for us (Gal. 3:13). It may be suggested that preachers study the commentaries on these Pauline passages, and use the Johannine text to proclaim a theology of the cross. In doing so they will be following the line, not of the Johannine redaction, but of the tradition that John used, similar in theology to Mark 15:34.

"It is finished" is not a good translation of the Johannine last word. The Greek is *tetelestai,* and NEB's "It is accomplished" strikes the right note. It is not a cry of despair but one of triumph. Mark perhaps intended the same thing when he said that "Jesus uttered a loud cry and breathed his last" (Mark 15:37). In fact, it is thought by some commentators that this cry is the only authentic historical tradition and that all the other words from the cross are articulations of it. Of the various ways of portraying Jesus on the cross, John, more than all the other evangelists, presents Jesus as reigning from the tree. John describes in his narrative the message of the triumphal crucifix, in which Jesus is presented crowned and clothed. In putting across this message, the preacher would be helped by Gustav Aulén's work entitled *Christus Victor.*

It has been argued by some scholars that there is really no logical place for the cross in Johannine theology and that the Passion narrative is included simply as a concession to tradition. This is because it is thought that John's whole emphasis is on the incarnation and on the revelation which the earthly Jesus brought. It is the incarnation, we are told, that saves us. In it Jesus is revealed as the way, the truth, and the life, and we need not know any more in order to attain to salvation, which is through revelation rather than redemption. It must be admitted that this interpretation appears to have its justification in the Johannine prologue with its climactic saying "The word became flesh and dwelt among us . . . we have beheld his glory" (John 1:14). From the prologue we should gather that the incarnation was sufficient to give us the power to become children of God (1:12) and to receive grace upon grace (1:16).

Attractive as this hypothesis may seem at first sight, it ignores much other important material in the Fourth Gospel. The word *flesh* in the prologue means not only the birth of Jesus but "his whole observable life," culminating in his death. It is there, in the whole of it, and especially in his death, that we see his glory. Moreover, just like Mark, John has planted signs which point to the cross right from the early chapters. In chapter 1, "Behold the Lamb of God" points to the cross. In chapter 2, Jesus assures his mother that his hour has not come yet, and thereby creates a tension that will last until the announcement in 13:1 that the last hour has come. After the wedding of Cana, Jesus goes to Jerusalem to cleanse the Temple—an episode evidently shifted by the Fourth Evangelist from just before the passion. Jesus declares that he replaces the Temple made with hands with the temple of his body—a clear pointer to the cross and resurrection.

This puts all the ensuing discourses under the sign of the cross. All that Jesus announces in the discourses about his identity and revelatory work, all his great "I am" sayings become true at the moment when he dies upon the cross. There for the first time, he really is all that he said he was: the bread that came down from heaven, the light of the world, the door, the good shepherd, the resurrection and the life, the way, the truth, and the life, the true vine. The text "It is accomplished" (NEB), could be expounded so as to bring out all of this.

The reading of the passion continues through the burial of Jesus. It is unlikely that the preacher will want to deal with this, except perhaps in passing, in the principal Good Friday service. But it would be particularly suitable as the subject for the address at an evening service on the same day.

The fact of Jesus' burial was part of the earliest kerygma (1 Cor. 15:4). Its function there was twofold. On the one hand it looked backward to the passion and death—the passion finally sealed his fate. He was not only dead but buried. The whole Jesus affair was at an end; the bottom line had been drawn. That was what the enemies of Jesus had set out to do and what, humanly speaking, they had succeeded in doing. But "he was buried" is followed in the earliest kerygma by the announcement that God raised Jesus from the dead. The burial is reversed: It also looks forward to the resurrection.

We have already called attention to another kerygmatic passage that interprets the burial of Jesus, not as an act of devotion by friends or sympathizers, but as a final act of rejection (Acts 13:29). That is probably the historical fact. We do not know for certain what kind of grave Jesus was buried in, for Paul tells us nothing about it, and the passage from Acts leaves us uncertain whether it was a common criminal's grave, as some have thought.

By the time the common Passion narrative took shape, the burial of Jesus had been reinterpreted as a friendly act by adherents or sympathizers. In the basic tradition this act was performed by Joseph of Arimathea. But in the tradition unique to the Johannine evangelist, there was a second version assigning the friendly role to Nicodemus, who is featured elsewhere in John (3:1–21; 7:50–52). The result is some overlapping of roles between the two characters, a sure sign of conflation. Nicodemus also duplicates the action of Mary of Bethany in chapter 12, for her action was declared to be in anticipation of Jesus' burial (12:7). Why has the Fourth Evangelist thus elaborated the story? The answer is probably that the description of the burial, "according to the custom of the Jews" prepares the way for the discovery of the grave cloths (John 20:4–8), which because of the way they are arranged enables the "other disciple" to come to faith. This means that the burial is designedly open-ended. The story of Jesus does not end with his burial but points forward to the denouement of Easter Day. It is fitting that the Good Friday observance should conclude on this note of waiting.

Traditionally, in Christian devotion, the burial of Jesus has been associated with the service of Compline, the last monastic office of the day. It included the following prayer, which will suggest a meditation combining the thought that going to bed each night is a reminder of our mortality with the thought that Jesus' burial is our hope of resurrection. The prayer reads as follows:

> O Lord Jesus Christ, who at this evening hour didst rest in the sepulchre, and didst thereby sanctify the grave to be a bed of hope to thy people; Make us so to abound in sorrow for our sins, which were the cause of thy passion, that when our bodies lie in the dust, our souls may live with thee; who livest and reignest with the Father and the Holy Spirit, one God, world without end. Amen.